Victorian Myths of the Sea

Rear-Admiral Sir Horatio Nelson, K.B., painted at Greenwich in 1797 after losing his arm at Teneriffe.
  L. F. Abbott

by permission
National Maritime Museum, Greenwich

Victorian Myths of the Sea

Cynthia Fansler Behrman

OHIO   UNIVERSITY   PRESS   :   ATHENS,   OHIO

"Big Steamers," copyright 1911 by Rudyard Kipling; "Song of the English," copyright 1909 by Rudyard Kipling, "The Islanders" and "The Last Chantey" from RUDYARD KIPLING'S VERSE, Definitive Edition. Reprinted by permission of the Executors of the Estate of Mrs. George Bambridge and Doubleday & Company, Inc.

Alfred Noyes' poem from his essay on "The Sea" reprinted by permission from the Estate of the late Dr. Alfred Noyes and William Blackwood & Sons Ltd.

For R.M.C.

Contents

Preface

THIS BOOK IS A DESCRIPTIVE ESSAY ABOUT A MYTH, OR, RATHER, A series of connected myths that are apparent in the last twenty years of the nineteenth century. It is my thesis that social myth stitches together the fabric of a culture and gives it the pattern or design that distinguishes it from other cultures. It is thus an important clue to the historian's understanding of that culture. My definition of the word *myth* appears in the first chapter. A hypercritical friend wrote me, "What you're doing is not history; it's closer to poetry." His comment startled me, because I should like history to be a bigger house than he will allow; it seems to me that the historical mansion can have many rooms not all of them public. Victorian homes usually had a drawing room (originally a "withdrawing room") for the family's use. To carry the metaphor a little further, I am trying to see what the members of the family are like in their drawing room, in their most private and least self-conscious moods.

The British political hegemony lasted roughly from about 1875 to the First World War. This was the period when the myths seemed most nearly coextensive with observable "fact." Grumble as they might, Germany and France and, to some extent, the United States had to submit to the actual superiority of the British navy. The myth of this superiority is traceable as far back as the eighteenth century and was given its strongest boost by the British victories in the Napoleonic period. But the popular culture seems to have awakened to the myth only when, in fact, the seeds of its destruction were being sown. I have, therefore, limited this study to the thirty years before 1914. One should remember, however, that men who were brought up in the high noon of Victoria were still feeling, thinking, acting, and directing policy during the war and afterwards. I have therefore not excluded postwar references where they were particularly illuminating.

Finally, a word must be said about a vexatious semantic problem. Strictly speaking *England* refers to a political entity, with *Eng-*

lish the adjective of reference. *Britain* as short for *Great Britain*, refers to an island and to the United Kingdom. Scots, Welshmen, and Northern Irish resent (understandably) the use of the term English where British is correct. It is the British navy, not the English navy, which dominated the seas in the nineteenth century. However, the English themselves are notoriously careless in their use of these adjectives, and while I shall endeavor to be exact, I cannot hope to avoid confusion altogether, especially when quoting directly.

I am grateful to the National Endowment for the Humanities and to the Faculty Research Fund of Wittenberg University for supporting the research for this study. I am also grateful to a host of friends and colleagues: to my husband for research assistance and unfailing encouragement; to Terry Otten, who understands both Victorian England and my understanding of it; to colleagues at Wittenberg, Berkeley, and elsewhere, who suffer my enthusiasms with tolerant forbearance; to the staffs of the Wittenberg University Library, the Ohio State University Library, the British Library, and the National Maritime Museum for kind and helpful assistance; and finally to the professor who sent me sailing down the uncharted seas of myth so many years ago.

Part 1

MYTH AND THE HISTORIAN

MAN CANNOT DO WITHOUT MYTH—THE VITAL, NECESSARY SOCIAL IN-gredient that gives meaning and order to our disorderly, sometimes frightening lives. Myth shapes our view of the universe, gives us goals, draws for us a self-image that allows us to contemplate existence without too much despair. Churchill built upon an English myth in the dark days of 1940: "We shall fight them on the beaches; we shall *never* give up." It scarcely matters that the English might *not* have had the courage to fight on the beaches; what mattered was that they should resist the German bombing with a spirit of community that would partly compensate for lack of ammunition. Such is the substance of myth. Sometimes if we think ourselves courageous, we muster enough bravery to face the tigers in the forest. Are Americans a freedom-loving, democratic, egalitarian, tolerant people? The fact is that we think ourselves so, and it is this myth that shapes so much of our perception of reality and helps to mold whatever guilts and pride we feel. I proceed with the two assumptions that myth is a necessary part of culture, and that myth is true.

1

The Nature of Myth

TOWARD A USEFUL DEFINITION

WHAT IS MYTH? THE WORD IS CONVENTIONALLY ASSOCIATED WITH classical Greeks and Romans and to a lesser extent with the cultural folk-literature of primitive peoples. Hercules performing prodigious feats, Prometheus contending with Zeus, Theseus with the Minotaur—these were the exciting myths of our childhood, explanations of natural phenomena, or dreams of glory and great deeds. Although, as our education in rational experience progressed, we came to accept the idea that the sun is not the chariot of a god and that the world does not sit on the back of a turtle, the early appeal of myth remained with us, now overlaid with the knowledge of its falsehood. To a child the "truth" of something is not really a relevant aspect of its being; he does not think of the myths of Hercules as either "true" or "untrue" in an adult sense, but only as something he likes or dislikes. As he grows older the adult world insists that he distinguish between what is true and false, and it inevitably forces him to develop a condescending attitude toward the untrue. Thus the *mythical* becomes in modern parlance *fictional*, a restriction that places upon myth the burden of proving itself as historical fact or running the risk of being tossed on the scrap heap of the trivial. In short, we have come to use *mythical* as a euphemism for *liar*, as a fifty-dollar word for *fictional*. I hope to demonstrate that the word *reality* is as legitimately a part of myth as it is a part of poetry. Myth partakes of a kind of social truth that has very little to do with reason or fact or empirical evidence. Our devout belief in the efficacy of the "true" fact—one of our legacies from the Enlightenment—has, I think, led us into the mischievous position of ignoring or depreciating the power of certain other kinds of knowledge. Man must "know," must discover to his own satisfaction the reasons for his existence, for his destiny, for his universe. He believes in order, for in order lies truth; in

3

truth, power and control. Because he has been falsely led astray by his belief in the sublime power of demonstrable fact he has, in the last two centuries, assumed that there was only one pathway to power, ignoring an important cultural phenomenon, a vital key to the understanding of any culture, that I propose to call myth.

I shall, then, define myth as a way of perceiving reality and, consequently, a way of imposing order upon the data of existence. To some extent, it serves religious functions: it consoles and explains. But myth is more than simply social belief, although often it has been studied solely in connection with religious performance. Robert Graves has defined myth as the reduction of ritual to narrative shorthand, tossing out of consideration all other legends, stories, tales, and folk histories that do not fit his definition. I should like to carry his idea a little further than he is willing to take it: all myth is the reduction to a narrative *or symbolic* shorthand of both ritual behavior and belief.[1] E. B. Tylor, a nineteenth-century ethnologist, saw the corpus of myth as lying somewhere between two fairly clearly defined districts of belief and unbelief and suggested that it was possible for each generation to transform and reshape the mythological themes of the past to make them more compatible with the right reason of its own time, as, for example, Plutarch's assuring his readers that the archaic story of Theseus would be made more historical by his (Plutarch's) own modifications.[2] A modern example might be the contribution of Freud to the Oedipus legend: his interpretation has so illumined corners of the old story that it is impossible today to think of Oedipus without considering Freud.

The Freudians professed to see in dreams, folktales, and myths an expression of wish fulfillment, on either the personal or the racial level. Freud insisted on characterizing childhood as the mirror of the primitive race, and he analyzed dreams as the expression of fantasy life not only of the individual but also of the society. Jung postulated the presence of "archetypes" or "myth-forming" structural elements in the unconscious psyche. He believed in the existence of a second psychic system of a collective, universal, and impersonal nature that is identical in all individuals. Jung categorically rejected the notion of myth as an allegorical interpretation of life. On the contrary, he thought that myths are the psychic life of the primitive, who *experiences* rather than *invents* them.[3] The particular contribution of the psychologists to our understanding of myth was their realization that human behavior is not only instrumental but symbolic: individual action is indirect as well as

4

direct in meaning. Any action, even the most trivial, has the capacity to become symbolic when it is repeated and when that repetition becomes self-conscious and deliberate; thus its connection with the linguistic symbol-making process becomes evident.

The intimacy between myth and history has interested many besides historians. Mircea Eliade, who has dwelt at length on the relationship, argues that myth is a form of religious experience. He calls myths "exemplar history" for the society in which they are preserved, although he emphasizes that we must remember it is not history in our usual sense of the word (that is, things that took place once and will not be repeated), but rather something that can be repeated, whose meaning and value lie in the repetition. Our common need "to prove," Eliade contends, shows the "importance primitive man attaches to things that *really happened*, to the events which actually took place in his surroundings: it shows how his mind hungers for what is 'real,' for what *is* in the fullest sense."[4] But why only primitive man? I think that we can see that the hunger is true of humanity as a whole, and in this sense every man is a protohistorian; he believes in the past, he searches for "proof," his mind hungers for what is "real." A conviction of reality is the very basic reassurance that the human mind needs in a slippery, deceptive world full of the pitfalls of experience where, as Gilbert and Sullivan sing, "Things are seldom what they seem." The fundamental fact of the search for history is the search for individual identity, for the certainty that truth *lies* in certainty, and that only through historical time—through event—can one be sure of existence. Proof of existence, if only historical existence, is reassuring. This fact is by no means startling; historians have been discussing history in this function for many years, but it is an important (and, I think, insufficiently considered) interpretation with respect to myth as exemplar history.

Bronislaw Malinowski remarks that myth is an indispensable ingredient of all culture, constantly regenerated: "Every historical change creates its mythology, which is, however, indirectly related to historical fact." Or, as he notes on a preceding page, myth is an active force, embodying its own reality which is just as real as any other verifiable reality.[5]

❋　　❋　　❋

Where is the historian indicated in this? Myth partakes of history, as we have seen. In primitive cultures (*primitive* in its most neutral sense) myth is protohistory, but it is not limited to this function. Myth is not solely euhemeristic in origin, and yet in many minds it has been inextricably confused with history, because its language tends to be historical. Furthermore, it often fulfills many of the same functions as history, but this is because history steps into the field of aesthetics (and rightfully so), and not because myth is trespassing. All written history has mythic elements and emotive functions that operate in a social context. Furthermore, all cultures have beliefs (religious and nonreligious) and attendant rituals that in turn have their explanatory, symbolic, and narrative myths. Just as the archeologist examines the artifact, the critic examines the poem, or the anthropologist the tribal dance, so must the historian examine the myths of the culture he is interested in, not as quaint examples of "false fact" but as a powerful social force, continually operative, continually in flux.

How he is to set about this task remains a difficult problem. For "traditional" history there is the established method: the search for the document; the collection, comparison, and verification of documents; and, finally, the interpretation of the information contained therein. But what constitutes the "documentation" of myth? I think we must agree with Eliade, Barnard, Lang, and a host of other scholars, that authentic myth is apt to be unconscious; we therefore must look for sources that are not, in general, explicit or avowedly mythmaking. Since a myth in the sense in which we have used it here is necessarily a collective rather than merely an individual belief, one can expect to find the culture's educational structure intimately involved in its inculcation. In a pluralistic Western society this will be a much larger field than the anthropologists have encountered in their Samoan puberty rites and the like, because all forms of persuasion are essentially educative, and in a literate society the sheer volume of the written word is staggering.

There is often, however, a cognitive difference between the *literary* culture and the *popular* culture. The literary culture is by definition more self-aware than the popular; to some extent, its myths are "pseudomyths" in that they are self-conscious ones; at least they are significantly different in their function. By and large, I have depended upon the sources of the popular culture for this study. I have not altogether ignored those of the literary culture, however. It seems to me that the two sometimes cross-fertilize each other: Tennyson, for example, was once a boy who was subject (as all children are) to the national myths. He could not have lost altogether the influence of these, even though as an adult he

6

became more aware of their affective quality. Similarly, the more popular poets and novelists themselves influenced the literary culture through the widespread circulation of the reviews, for example, and (particularly after 1890) the new journalism of the popular press.

Generally speaking, it is true of myth that it follows a sine curve over time through the history of a particular culture. The historian, therefore, may either follow the path of this curve, demonstrating and describing the myth as it grows and then wanes; or he might make a lateral slice through the culture, so to speak, seeing in operation several overlapping myths, each at a different point in its life. We must, furthermore, contemplate—indeed, acknowledge and embrace—the possibility that the elucidation may become part of the text, as in Freud's Oedipus, for example, or as in one of those Saul Steinberg drawings of an artist sketching, where one follows the pictured artist's hand back to wrist and arm only to discover that they are part of the picture being drawn. The myth then is both prediction and fulfillment, or, as Georges Sorel described it, the framing of the future, the body of images capable of evoking instinctively the appropriate necessary sentiments.[6]

Part 2

THE MYTHS OF THE SEA

THE SUBJECT OF THIS STUDY IS THE MYTHS OF THE SEA IN LATE-Victorian England. Certain myths in the popular culture were striking: the English people, by virtue of their history and racial inheritance had more moral right than other nations to decide the destiny of seafaring countries; England, an island, was separate both geographically and psychologically from Europe and the rest of the world (a separation which conveyed special rights and privileges); the English seaman, because he came of seafaring folk, was a prototype of the best of the race: courageous, moral, upright, strong, tolerant, and just; the British navy patrolled the seven seas and had to be God's agent on the ocean, because it was the only force that could be expected to act disinterestedly for the world's benefit. There were, of course, minor myths attendant upon these major ones. Accordingly, I have divided the study into three major sections: the English self-image, the English seaman, and the role of the navy.

2

The English Romance with the Sea

I must down to the seas again, to the lonely sea and the sky
And all I ask is a tall ship and a star to steer her by
. . . .
I must down to the seas again, for the call of the running tide
Is a wild call and a clear call that may not be denied

Masefield

Who hath desired the Sea?—the sight of salt water unbounded—
The heave and the halt and the hurl and the crash of the comber wind-
     hounded?

Kipling

MASEFIELD'S LINES, SO FAMILIAR THAT THEY ARE ALMOST TRITE,
reflect the deep and intimate English love affair with the sea. The
sea symbolism found in the later Victorian period had roots much
earlier in the century in the Romantics' preoccupation with mythic
material for literature, and even in the eighteenth-century fondness
for sea ballads of all kinds. But the intimacy of man and sea seemed
to reach a peak in late-Victorian times, when national power and
policy, articulate public enthusiasm, and fortunate circumstances
combined to reinforce and promote the myths of the sea. There
are many levels at which one might look at these myths; levels
on which myth is perceived and effective, but I shall start with
fundamental, unconscious feelings before examining their application on the level of explicit behavior and thought. Accordingly,
in this chapter I shall deal with the romance of the sea: the psychology of the lure of the sea, or "sea-fever," as Masefield called
it. From there I shall look at the English sense of history that directly reflected and intensified the myths.

When considering man's relationship to nature, one is continually struck by how often man forces nature to become an organizing principle for his own perception of reality. He tames the amorphous universe, forcing it to bear the weight of whatever symbolic importance he places upon it. Thus the land becomes the Garden; the sky the Heavens; the wild beast the King of the Animals. By mythologizing a power, man fancies he can control it. "If God did not exist, it would be necessary to invent him," Voltaire said. Man needs meaning in his life. Through order comes meaning; through knowledge of order comes control. There is great security in the awareness of power, even superhuman power. Even unpredictability becomes predictable and therefore less frightening by the very fact of acknowledging its randomness. Thus the senseless has a certain sense and the thirst for meaning is assuaged.

This process of transmuting an element from the natural to the symbolic operates with water, too. Man's physiological dependence upon water is basic, and his metaphoric dependence upon it significant. Water functions symbolically in many of his ceremonies, in much of his liturgy and cosmology, and in his language. Water metaphors run in a constant thread through the fabric of Victorian writing, prose (fiction, essays, and sermons) as well as poetry. Jerome Buckley in *The Victorian Temper*, discusses in his chapter "The Pattern of Conversion" this pervasive quality of the water image, citing popular novels from Kingsley's *The Water-Babies* through Dickens's *David Copperfield, Hard Times, Great Expectations*; to George Eliot's *The Mill on the Floss* and *Romola*. He points out that water is the instrument of baptism and betokens not only the acceptance of the soul into the communion of God but also a spiritual regeneration and rebirth. He mentions in this connection the very characteristic evangelical symbolic cleansing that was sacramental and ritual and a constant theme in Victorian Christianity.[1] But redemption meant death before rebirth. The symbolic association of the sea with death was inevitable, not only because the sea was the literal grave of so many, but also, in a far more compelling way than on land, burial at sea would mean reabsorption of the individual life into the greater life process, the eternal Source. "At Midnight of All Souls," a poem by a minor Victorian writer, Mary Cowden Clarke, exhibits these images in profusion:

> I hear the rushing of the sea of Time,
> Whose mighty waters in their pauseless whelm,
> Suck down, resistless, nation, race, and realm,

Like rotting sea-weed, drench'd in ooze and slime.
Ocean! incarnadin'd with countless crime,
Green with drown'd hopes, and wreck of joyous prime;
Salt with myriad tears of human woes;
Toss'd with the surge and tumult of earth's throes;
We note thy shifting sands, and pace the shore,
We watch thy ebbing tides, and list thy roar,
Heark'ning, with awe, th'innumerable things
Told in thy billowing thunderings;
Until by the coming of our one appointed wave,
We're swept into th'eddy of that universal grave.[2]

Water could symbolize, then, both directly and indirectly, the cleansing of the soul from sin and the challenge of the Christian God for redemption and regeneration. The living ˋwater through which one is refreshed and reborn was a recurrent theme. Salt water is somewhat special; although it partakes of many of the qualities assigned to water in general, there are a number of roles which it plays alone. To begin with, of course, although it is buoyant, salt water is inhospitable. It provides food, but it cannot sustain human life. The sea, having no end, no limits, no markers, becomes the very flow of life in which any markers are merely arbitrary, man-made things. Water in the form of the infinite sea thus takes on another religious quality in symbolizing an eternal process of life. Hopkins's poem "The Wreck of the *Deutschland*" uses the circumstance of nautical disaster to exemplify the majesty and wisdom of God, and the sea represents both the suffering of mankind and the source of his ultimate redemption. For a nation surrounded by salt water and dependent upon it for livelihood, it is understandable that the sea would take on a special significance and develop its own specific myth.

Probably the best way of looking at this aspect of the sea-myth is through the more explicit mythmakers. As I have noted, the literary culture is apt to be much more aware of what it is doing than the popular. For example, if an editor collects, anthologizes, and publishes all the sea poetry he can find, both good and bad, he will be contributing to the extension of the myth in some relation to the popularity of the book. The process is important: Kipling's poetry and stories were well known and very popular in his day: whole generations of British children learned to recite "If—" and to sing "The Recessional." Schoolboys read Marryat and Conrad; their parents read Arnold and Swinburne or sang "Spanish Ladies" around the piano after dinner. The literary or aesthetic quality of the mythic source, therefore, will not be of major interest here.

Among the most articulate of those who attempted to express what was for many an inexpressible relationship was Joseph Conrad. It is perhaps ironic that one of the most moving expressions of the English love affair with the sea should have come from the pen of a Pole, but this illustrates the fact that the absorption of myth is a learned experience.

Conrad himself was both mythmaker and victim of myth. From his native Poland he joined the British merchant marine, much to the dismay of his family. He had conceived a desire to try sea life, inspired by his reading and by a visit to the shipyards and docks at Marseilles. His own life at sea followed a usual pattern: he served in the merchant marine, passed his examination for an officer's license (for which he had to learn English very thoroughly), and spent many years roaming over the globe, absorbing the flavor not only of the nautical life but also of the English attitudes toward empire and the rest of the world.

Conrad apparently was an avid reader of the works of Captain Marryat, an early-nineteenth-century nautical novelist. He once wrote of Marryat, "He is the enslaver of youth, not by the false glamour of presentation, but by the heroic quality of his own unique temperament."[3] Conrad extolled the spirit and animation of Marryat's work and his fidelity to the service and profession of the navy. The same might be said with even more justification of Conrad's own work. He finally retired from the ocean to write stories worthy of the Marryat tradition (but far superior to Marryat's work), stories that surely influenced many a young mind to turn to the "senior service."

In 1906 Conrad published *The Mirror of the Sea*, in which he discussed and analyzed the lure of the sea felt by himself and so many of his adopted countrymen. It is a collection of reminiscences and reflective essays on his relationship to the sea in his long career as a seaman and an officer in the merchant marine, a relationship he described as a "great passion."[4] Clearly he was a little embarrassed by this passion and rather defensive about it. Some people might scoff and call it, rather, a "foolish infatuation," but he reminds us that those words have always been applied to other persons' love affairs, not to one's own. In his preface he described his book as "the best tribute my piety can offer to the ultimate shapers of my character, convictions, and in a sense, destiny—to the imperishable sea, to the ships that are no more, and to the simple men who have had their day."[5] His words sum up what was felt very deeply by less articulate people, because for many Englishmen

14

their relationship with the imperishable sea and all its qualities was one closely akin to that of a passionate love affair. Indeed one can see many of the common characteristics of sexual love in the imagery and the diction of writers both well known and obscure who undertook to describe the sea and all its various moods and manifestations.

First of all the sea was always female in parlance. "The sea, fire, and women are three evils" was a proverb of the ancient Greeks, according to one anthologist.[6] The sea, like a woman, was unpredictable and uncontrollable. Her other qualities could also be considered "female," at least to the conventional mid- and late-Victorian view: a certain restless wildness, emotional fervor and passion, and strange mystery, always a little beyond the grasp of man's understanding. Recent writers have suggested that one of the reasons why men were so firm in their insistence on woman's place was precisely that they feared the unleashing of femaleness, of a power that surpassed men's power and that therefore needed to be kept in check by rigid conventions of "femininity." The essence of mystery is that it must transcend human understanding: one may try to know it, one may learn a tiny corner of it, but one is never able to encompass the whole. This is both its attraction and its terror.

But beyond the force of mystery there is the sheer physical power of the sea. Man's attitude toward this power has varied from awe at its implacability to the belief that it has a malevolent, mysterious will behind it. Conrad in the space of a few pages wrote at first as though the ocean were a friend to those faithful to it and then remarked on its cynical indifference to virtue and vice alike, swallowing up ships and men with total unconcern for the morality of the action:

He—man or people—who, putting his trust in the friendship of the sea, neglects the strength and cunning of his right hand, is a fool! As if it were too great, too mighty for common virtues, the ocean has no compassion, no faith, no law, no memory. Its fickleness is to be held true to men's purposes only by an undaunted resolution, and by a sleepless, armed, jealous vigilance, in which, perhaps, there has always been more hate than love.[7]

This attitude is very similar to that of primitive man toward his deities. Sir James Frazer in his description of the primitive's use of magic pointed up this same feeling: man's relationship to power is always that of supplicant. Gods are strong, but they are generally indifferent to man's needs. Although not usually malevolent, their interest in man is fleeting and it takes constant attention to turn their power to man's welfare. Even then one is not always successful. The sea becomes, therefore, a spirit to be known, to be won, to be placated.

Conrad told an interesting story of what he called his "initiation" into the wisdom of the sea. Once his ship came across a sinking brig with a few people on board. His own ship had lost wind and was unable to reach the sinking vessel in time, so the boats were lowered. Conrad described the race against death for a prize of nine men's lives, a weird rescue, as he put it, in which his men pitted their strength against the voraciousness of the sea. They won the race and rescued the men only a few minutes before the brig sank. Here is Conrad's analysis.

> On that exquisite day of gentle breathing peace and veiled sunshine perished my romantic love to what men's imagination had proclaimed the most august aspect of Nature. The cynical indifference of the sea to the merits of human suffering and courage, laid bare in this ridiculous, panic-tainted performance extorted from the extremity of nine good and honourable seamen, revolted me. I saw the duplicity of the sea's most tender mood. It was so because it could not help itself, but the awed respect of the early days was gone. I felt ready to smile bitterly at its enchanting charm and glare viciously at its furies. In a moment, before we shoved off, I had looked coolly at the life of my choice. Its illusions were gone, but its fascination remained, I had become a seaman at last.[8]

In that one short experience he had grown from infatuated adolescent to mature lover, from the love that is blind to the destructive power of the beloved to the love that accepts, realistically, the danger of the relationship. He had looked upon the "true" sea, "the sea that plays with men until their hearts are broken, and wears stout ships to death."[9] On the sea nothing can touch the brooding bitterness of its soul, open to all and faithful to none, whose love cannot be plighted, who has no obligation and no fidelity, but whose fascination is irresistible once it seizes men's minds.

Many other writers also expressed this quality of inevitability in the relationship of man to the sea. One of Swinburne's poems called "The Return" begins,

I will go back to the great sweet mother,
Mother and lover of men, the sea.
I will go down to her, I and none other,
Close with her, kiss her, and mix her with me.

There is an inexorable contradiction in the relationship: woman is both mother and lover. As the one, she will cherish; as the other she will deceive and perhaps betray. In the first role the sea is the great womb, the ultimate security; in the second, she is fickle, untrustworthy, cruel. The contrast expresses the same kind of Victorian ambivalence toward so much of life: life that intrigues, that calls, but is full of danger for the unwary pilgrim. It is difficult (but I think justifiable) to ignore Swinburne's own psychosexual bent in this context. The sentiments are common enough to warrant inclusion. In Swinburne's poem there is that quality of the child seeking redemption and justification, constantly placating the enemy while at the same time wishing to become one with the enemy. The attitude of the child to the unpredictable moods of the parent, the alternating tenderness and cherishing qualities of Mother, and the angry, storm-provoking qualities of avenging Father (probably very well known to Victorian childhood), changes constantly. First the child appeases powers whose mysterious qualities are beyond him, and then he surrenders to the overpowering wrath which annihilates and devours him.

One of Kipling's poems, "The Song of the Dead," is centered on the idea of the voracious sea:

We have fed our sea for a thousand years
And she calls us, still unfed.

And "Song of the Sea" by William Watson ends with the lines:

For in mine hour of wrath no ruth have I,
Ev'n I the tempest-hearted pitiless sea.

But there is also the soothing maternal sea in Sir Henry Taylor's poem, where he

Hears the low plash of wave o'erwhelming wave,
The loving lullaby of mother ocean.[10]

The examples could be multiplied.

This schizoid image of mother-lover could be seen in a number of places. Many times writers would refer to the "call of the sea" as though it were some irresistible siren voice. H. E. Acraman Coate, the author of *Realities of Sea Life: Describing the Duties, Prospects, and Pleasures of a Young Sailor in the Merchant Marine*, related that the sea called him every spring until he finally was old enough to join the merchant marine. It is not without significance that he claimed to have been brought up on the works of Marryat and W. Clark Russell, two very popular nautical novelists. In his preface he made the interesting point that the purpose of his book was not only to encourage this love of the sea but to be very realistic about the hardships of a seafaring life. He clearly believed in Conrad's idea that the sea desires devoted lovers, not merely capricious fools whose heads have been turned by romantic nonsense.[11]

Conrad wrote of man's relationship to the sea through the medium of a symbolic equivalent of the sea, namely, the ship. This is a curious juxtaposition of metaphor and yet one that has a great deal of meaning for an understanding of this strange relationship between man and sea. Like the sea, the ship was feminine: in some ways a symbolic microcosm of the ocean itself, but one that had been tamed, that man could master, provided he had the key to her mysteries. In many places the ship symbolized society or social order. Collective, or social, man was on a journey, and the ship represented an ordered world facing the chaotic and the disordered. Familiar phrases such as "ship of fools" and "ship of state" illustrate how trite is the image. (The ship is also the microcosm of society in law, too, in that the captain has many legal powers on the high seas, where he functions as the leader and judge.) No doubt the image is largely utilitarian, but the coincidence of idea is perhaps significant. In most places, however, the ship is personified, and the relationship is a much more individual one. Again Conrad wrote, "Your ship wants to be humoured with knowledge. You must treat with an understanding consideration the mysteries of her feminine nature, and then she will stand by you faithfully in the unceasing struggle with forces, wherein defeat is no shame. It is a serious relation, that in which a man stands to his ship. She has her rights, as though she could breathe and speak; and, indeed, there are ships that, for the right man, will do anything but speak, as the saying goes." He made a similar point in a short story, "The Secret Sharer," where the narrator, a ship's captain, sees life on the sea with his ship as straightforward, elemental, and secure. This story is full of Jungian male-female symbolism.[12]

But Conrad went on to say that the ship is not a slave. She will work for you faithfully, provided you give her the fullest share of your thought, your skill, your love, your tenderness, your devotion. Still, one can never fully know a ship. Ships vary; they have as many idiosyncrasies as people. A certain mystery hangs over the ship, the same kind, although to a smaller degree, as the sea itself holds for mankind. But (and here the metaphor falters) the sea is unknowable where the ship is knowable. The ship responds to man's care, to man's devotion; she is, to some extent, fickle and unpredictable, but her qualities are always ultimately within man's grasp. If the sea is the wildest goddess-mistress of Poseidon, the ship is the domesticated hearth goddess—the wife. She is also the instrument of truth, bringing out the otherwise hidden qualities of man, weaknesses as well as strengths. Conrad, for example, told story after story where a ship's peculiarities were the medium for exposing an incompetent captain or mate. After one such tale he drew this moral: "Yet the answer was clear. The ship had found out the momentary weakness of her man. Of all the living creatures upon land and sea, it is ships alone that cannot be taken in by barren pretenses, that will not put up with bad art from their masters."[13] This particular captain had been guilty of thinking of his own selfish glory, of wanting a showy performance that would redound to his own credit. The ship showed him up for what he was.

But while the ship was an incorruptible agent to test man's evil qualities, she would repay commitment and service. The seaman who devoted himself to her welfare and to the greater welfare of all his fellows, who was totally unselfish and gave his very best to the ship's service, was amply rewarded in the service she rendered to him. However there could be no pretense or falseness and no swerving from the art and love that she required. Interestingly, one reason some people regretted the switch from sail to steam in the navy was that it would eliminate, so they thought, some of this craft that the seaman owed to his ship. They felt that the machine interposed its mechanical impersonality in the relationship between man and nature, and fatefully altered the character of the struggle between them. Conrad himself, who was brought up in the sailing era (although he had experience with both kinds of vessels), deplored the introduction of steam and the obsolescence of sail. The special call of an art that passed away could never be

19

reproduced, he felt, and nothing would awaken the same emotional response. The sailing of a modern steamship is less personal, less arduous; perhaps more precise but less gratifying in the lack of "close communion between the artist and the medium of his art. It is, in short, less a matter of love."[14]

What was gone, of course, was one major element of unpredictability in man's relationship with his ship and with his destination: the wind. The wind power of the sailing vessel could not be counted on and could be predicted only inaccurately; it was a fickle and troublesome master, never a servant. The wind itself, like so many elements connected with the sea, was anthropomorphic. We hear, for example, of the "angry wind" or "sullen tempest" or "gentle breeze," all suggesting human will and emotion beyond these forces of nature. These were by no means impersonal, except that they had an amoral quality to them and were indifferent to the human demands of morality. When they claimed a victim, they were as likely to seize the just as the unjust. They were thus a kind of junior partner to the sea. Conrad's section on winds is intriguing. He wrote of the competition and ultimate truce between the East wind and the West wind, with the West wind the undisputed monarch of the kingdoms of the earth. The North wind and the South wind were insignificant; they were but "small princes in the dynasties that make peace and war upon the sea." The real struggle lay between East and West. Conrad considered the West wind supreme and more terrifying primarily because it is the wind that reigns over the seas surrounding the British Isles. The whole section of some ten or twelve pages on the winds, the rulers of east and west, as he called them, is fraught with a kind of pantheist superstition that is more than petty and primitive but wild and mysterious in its grandeur.[15]

It is, of course, a cliché that the sailor is superstitious, but I wonder if Conrad was not simply expressing fears that all humans would feel if their lives involved confrontation with the fury and force of natural elements like the wind and the sea. Certainly man's ability to deal with these forces develops in direct proportion to his knowledge of them, and his inclination to invest the world with spirits—malevolent as well as beneficent—is an expression of his need to know.

The ship, finally (steam or sail), symbolized life itself. The feeling was explicit in many of the narratives of boys who ran away to sea, who clearly visualized the act as one of running *toward* life. The ship was thus not only the metaphor of man's relationship to the forces of nature, it became man himself, expressing the motion of life, sailing the seas forever. The metaphor is related to the theme of rites of passage, as in the *bildungs-roman* of the youth who must earn his identity, and also to the figure of the ship's voyage as a pilgrimage. As Buckley remarks, you see this expression of life as a ship in Tennyson. In one of his poems, "The Voyage," he developed the simile of the sea journey as a pilgrimage that demands fortitude and steadfastness from the seaman. "And never sail of ours was furl'd," says Tennyson, "Nor anchor dropt at eve or morn," and the poem ends with the lines

> We know the merry world is round,
> And we may sail for evermore.

The word "merry" is ironic; the endless journey inevitably suggests monotony as well as inexorable quality of infinity.[16]

The theme of the voyage, the quest, or the journey was also an ancient one. Tennyson's version of the Ulysses myth illustrates the same kind of restless, brooding, driven quality that we see so often in English sea literature. In this poem the journey becomes one of dedication, of searchings: "'Tis not too late to seek a newer world. . . . To sail beyond the sunset." And finally, "To strive, to seek, to find, and not to yield." The journey, therefore, is a constant challenge, full of danger; a journey in which man's individual worth, virtue, skill, devotion, courage, and moral rectitude are no guarantees of his reaching an ultimate destination. But then, life itself is like that. The Victorians gloried in the idea of constant challenge and constant sacrifice; hence the post-Enlightenment preoccupation with Becoming rather than Being. The devotion of a whole life might still not suffice to gain desired redemption, but still it was necessary to struggle, for it was the journey, not the arrival, that mattered. In this fact may lie the Victorian modernity of the myth, as opposed to the traditional myths of the sea that stress finality and "endings."

❈   ❈   ❈

We have, therefore, the sea filling the religious role at many particular and varied levels. The sea, through its agent, the ship, can test man's ability, can prove him and expose his folly. The sea also can be an agent for conversion, for baptism, and regeneration. But there is a final level, perhaps more wild and primitive, in

21

which the sea functioned in a religious context. The sea was full of mystery. Again and again she would startle man with her caprice, with the way she sacrificed one and spared another; or she would surprise him with her tempests and calms, her wildness and serenity, her changeableness. She was mysterious and infinite. It was this sense of the infinite that was so overwhelming. Conrad wrote about it again and again, either explicitly or implicitly. In his first chapter, "Land Falls and Departures," he told of the difference between a mere leaving of port and a real departure. While land remains in sight, as when a ship sails down a coast, she has not really made a departure. But once she has gone beyond the sight of land, with only the open sea and the open sky to confront her, then she has made her departure. Then the sailor and the ship are alone, facing that mysterious Consciousness that controls the universe. The emptiness, the wilderness of the sea is so vast, so universal, that its awe-inspiring character has forced man to attempt—through his myths and theologies—to account for and to come to terms with the infinite.

For the sea represents all: beauty, power, quest, redemption, searching, life, healing, soothing, conquering. It is, one might say, the ultimate metaphor, and exerts (it is impossible to disbelieve these writers) the most overpowering influence on both mariner and landsman; on all who come within the sorcery of her sway.

These were not exclusively Victorian feelings, to be sure, but they were so pronounced in the sources of the late nineteenth century that they inevitably affected the myths of the navy and the seaman, building and promoting a sense of proprietorship. As a more literate society reads more it reacts more. As a more democratic society learns more of its heritage it creates more myths. And when Kipling asked the question, "Who hath desired the Sea?— the sight of salt water unbounded—the heave and the halt and the hurl and the crash of the comber wind-hounded?" the answer was automatic. Who hath desired the sea? The sea's people, the English people. The lure and the spell and the sway of her magic were inexorable—and unmistakable.

Did the English feel this more than other people whose livelihood depends on the sea? Possibly not, but it is clear that they thought they did. Much of the possessiveness that the English expressed about the sea was reflected in and reinforced by their sense of history, to which we must turn next. One function of history is to provide a people with a sense of identity. The need of a people for history is closely akin to its need for a community of myth, as described in chapter 1. George Eliot cogently expressed this need: "The eminence, the nobleness of a people depends on its capability of being stirred by memories, and of striving for what we call spiritual ends—ends which consist not in immediate material possession, but in the satisfaction of a great feeling that animates the collective body as with one soul."[17] It is, therefore, in the history of a people—not the "real" history but the history of learned belief—that one will find the most intense myths, the most cherished pictures of the national self-image, whose acceptance provides Eliot's "collective animation."

3

The English Sense of History

"When I use a word," Humpty Dumpty said, in a rather
scornful tone, "it means just what I choose it to mean."

Lewis Carroll

ALTHOUGH MYTH IS NOT SYNONYMOUS WITH HISTORY, THE TWO ARE
intimately connected. The critic Cleanth Brooks hit on the happy
phrase "history without footnotes" to describe the role of Keats's
Grecian urn. A professional historian might quarrel with Brooks's
evident assumption that real history is mere names-and-dates, but
his explanation of the "Sylvan historian" comes close to what we
mean here by mythic history—what he terms a "valid perception
into reality."[1]

As history organizes and gives meaning to the past, so myth
organizes the present and past. But myth must build on a knowledge of the past and hence must depend on some given perception
of historical event in order to shape its own data. For example,
when the English assumed a racial and ethnic superiority over
other peoples, they naturally looked to their past to discover evidence which supported this belief. Thus the history learned in
school and out would become mythic to the extent that it provided
this evidence. Ultimately, one might say, it scarcely matters what
"actually happened" in the past; what people think happened is
what their actions are based upon. I do not mean to say there is
never such a thing as "truth" in history; rather I suggest that truth
is not an operative element when one is dealing with mythic history. (Once more, I must caution the reader that the opposite is
not necessarily true: because we say that the mythic is not empiri-
cally true, it does not follow that it is therefore false.)

This Panglossian view of one's past, where everything turns out

24

THE ENGLISH SENSE OF HISTORY

for the best, was very characteristic of English (and American) historiography in the nineteenth century. By a fine chop of logic "defeat" was defined as "victory," and England's enemies were pressed into service as her own heroes. The naval mutiny of 1799 proved that sailors had pluck; the cowardice of Admiral Byng pointed up the everyday bravery of the majority; all exceptions proved the rule. Such an attitude turned accident into act of God and used temporary setback to give depth and character to ultimate triumph. J. K. Laughton, for example, claimed that the Americans won their independence because, luckily, the British navy at the time was weak with political graft and jobbery. The outcome was a good thing for the futures of both countries.[2] A book titled *Stirring Sea Fights: A Book for British Boys* described the glorious battle in 1591 between Sir Richard Grenville and the Spanish, at odds of one to fifty-three. Grenville's refusal to surrender early and his courageous trip to Spain to plead for the lives of his men turned a defeat into a moral victory, since Spain agreed to his terms. The whole chapter reads as though this were a page in a narrative of English naval successes! A work of this genre that is probably far better known is Tennyson's "Charge of the Light Brigade," a poem which, incidentally, employed many sea images.

History as a collection of agreed-upon assumptions about the past thus becomes the medium through which myth is promoted and taught, and the two become vitally interdependent. Many of the clichés about England's racial skill with ships, her superior navy, and her place among the nations on the high seas are directly traceable to the historical base which underlies the formation of myth. If we look at Victorian history, therefore, we shall see reflected the nation's self-image and find important elements of the English sea mythology. We shall see not only the source and formation of myth, but the substance itself. History, here, will be considered in a rather broad definition.

There are two ways in which the influence of history affected the sea-myths in the late-Victorian period: (1) in the self-image of the Englishman and (2) in his image of other peoples. Certainly the most prominent element of the first was the English assumption of ownership of the seas. In 1878 Robert Louis Stevenson wrote that the Englishman had a natural possessive feeling about the sea. He thought that every nation needed a symbol—like the Roman eagle—a particular sign of patriotic glory and success that would give individuals the feeling that they were part of a larger whole, give them a sense of unity without which national success is im-

25

possible. If an Englishman wished to point to such an emblem, he would find it not in the royal lion, which had never been "naturalized" as an English symbol, but instead would hit on the sea: "The sea is our approach and bulwark; it has been the scene of our greatest triumphs and dangers, and we are accustomed in lyrical strains to claim it as our own."[3]

Stevenson conceded somewhat wryly that to suppose yourself endowed with a natural affinity for the sea and nautical skill just because you were the countryman of Blake or mighty Nelson was perhaps as silly and unwarranted as to imagine that Scottish descent meant that you looked good in a kilt. But he goes on to say (and this is indeed the theme of this whole book) that feelings are often beyond the reach of rational argument, and to attempt to approach them that way is unprofitable: "We should consider ourselves unworthy of our descent if we did not share the arrogance of our progenitors, and please ourselves with the pretension that the sea is English. Even where it is looked upon by the guns and battlements of another nation we regard it as a kind of English cemetery, where the bones of our seafaring fathers take their rest until the last trumpet; for I suppose no other nation has lost as many ships, and sent as many brave fellows to the bottom."[4] (The thought that a graveyard becomes the possession of its inmates is interesting and was apparently a prevalent one. Compare, for example, Rupert Brooke's poem "The Soldier" of forty years later about the dead English recruit who, by the very presence of his body, sanctifies foreign soil and makes it English.)

The author of *The Boy's Life of Nelson* cribbed directly from Stevenson's article in *Cornhill*. Stevenson had commented that the English, unlike the Romans and other nations, were unusual in that they did not, as a rule, make imaginary allies out of the forces of nature. J. Cuthbert Hadden, however, took Stevenson's idea a step further, claiming that while England did not ally herself to mythic animal forces, she did get the same feeling of linkage with the eternal from her kinship with the sea that the Romans got from eagles: "It might almost be said, indeed, that from the sea only can such a feeling be obtained."[5]

Stevenson accounted for this possessiveness by saying it came from a romantic contemplation of past heroism and the fantastic beauty of the old warships. He thought that all Englishmen thrilled to the tune of heroic sacrifice; to the horror of the cruelty, dirt, and insane tyranny of naval service in the bad old days; and thus they felt proud that officers and men—bold and honest fellows that they were—managed to rise above their unspeakable living conditions. Overpowering glory pitted against overwhelming odds has an appeal all its own, but surely he was begging the question here. Other nations had lost brave men; other nations had beautiful ships; and other nations, too, had treated their seamen poorly, some even worse than the English. Perhaps the answer is simply that any seagoing nation, surrounded by water and (at least in the modern period) dependent upon seagoing trade to support life, will make a virtue out of a necessity and claim the ocean as its natural right. The interesting thing is that Stevenson (who represented the feelings of many others, as we shall see) seemed convinced by his own arguments—by his apparent belief that the English *were* more heroic, that the English had lost more men, and that the English were more impressed by courageous sacrifice than other people. Even were it so, we should again have to ask the question, Why?

The answer may be found in the Victorian historical imagination. The connection between the sea and history was a close one, and if the sea could symbolize life it also could symbolize the infinite flow of history, which in one sense was the narrative of that life. As the journalist and military expert Spenser Wilkinson wrote, "What gives the sea its historical significance is its continuous extent. Though it has different names in different parts, it is one single uninterrupted surface. . . . This is the secret of the sea. It is of infinite purport, for it implies some kind of community between all mankind."[6] But the idea can be just as credibly expressed in reverse fashion: for the Englishman it was his history which gave the sea its significance. It, too, seemed to be of infinite purport; it, too, provided a sense of community, if not of all mankind, at least of the present with the past. When he could feel the jointed chain of self, stretching forward as well as back, the chain in which his own times were but a single link, it gave him the same sense of order and purpose that Stevenson meant when he was talking of lions and eagles.

In one popular history for children, the author discussed this quality of possession, which he considered racial in origin. "The love of the restless ocean implanted in the hearts of our fierce piratical ancestors has never quite left the British boy," he says, and no matter where a British child grows up—in smoky industrial city or inland farm—his racial love of the sea will be with him, to help make him "look upon the blue waters as his especial birthright." A superpatriot, schoolteacher, and sometime Social Darwinist made virtually the same comment in an essay on English citizenship when he talked of "the love of the sea inherent in the breasts of a people, sprung from a race whose greatest exploits of conquest and adventure have been intimately associated with seamanship." He believed in "glorious history" which justified and explained all racial and national pride. Professional historians expressed similar beliefs: E. A. Freeman once described the English as "folk of the sea, to whom the sea is a true home," and James Anthony Froude called the sea the "natural home of the Englishman."[7]

Poets, too, claimed possession. In "A Word for the Nation" Swinburne called the English "lords of the sea;" and Tennyson, celebrating the arrival of Princess Alexandra of Denmark, who was about to be married to the Prince of Wales in 1863, saluted her as a "Sea-king's daughter from over the sea" and expressed the graceful hope that she would feel at home in her new land because the English and the Danes were racially so close ("Saxon and Norman and Dane are we"), all children of the sea. In a much more famous poem "The Fleet," written some twenty years later, Tennyson called England "This isle, the mightiest Ocean-power on earth,/Our own fair isle, the lord of every sea—." Or one might quote Kipling, who wrote a poem called "The Last Chantey" in 1892 on the biblical quotation "And there was no more sea." The poem centers on the idea that when the smoke of Judgment Day cleared and the earth had passed away, the Lord decided that He would also gather up the sea. But in several stanzas the various "jolly, jolly mariners" protest and argue respectfully that God should spare the sea. "Give us back the sea," the mariners (obviously the English) cry, and so in the last stanza

> Sun, Wind, and Cloud shall fail not from the face of it,
> Stinging, ringing, spindrift, nor the fulmar flying free;
> And the ships shall go abroad
> To the Glory of the Lord
> Who heard the silly sailor-folk and gave them back their sea!

The sailor-folk may be silly (that is, simple-minded), but the Lord indulges them their fancy, which fact suggests that they must have some influence with Him.

This notion that somehow the Lord plays favorites with nations is not peculiar to the British. One can probably dig up the image of "chosen people" in every civilized society. For the Victorian, God's favor seemed to come as a direct result of superior virtue, and proof of His benignity could be found by anyone who cared to look at the record of the past. Superior virtue on the national level required superior virtue on a personal level. Squire Brown wanted his son Tom to grow up to be a truth-telling, Christian gentleman, and *Tom Brown's School-Days* became the epitome of the Victorian ideal in the latter part of the century. It was no wonder, then, that a school textbook could say of India in all seriousness, "No native trusts another as he trusts the bare word of a sahib. Our truthfulness, our evident desire to be fair, our moral as well as physical courage form the prestige that makes a single unarmed Briton master among a million of vassals." By and large it is a complacent image, but it had its difficulties. No parent claimed that it was easy to follow the path of virtue, and children were constantly warned of the sin of pride and of the temptations of the devil. A fellow of the Royal Geographical Society, who wrote a series of sketches to promote interest in the sea, claimed that the English were paradoxical creatures: efficient but muddling, generous but stingy, a "turbulent, restless race, impatient with restraint . . . the true stuff of which empires are builded," and "the greatest nation of peaceful traders the world has ever seen."[8] By acknowledging the negative as well as the positive qualities he could get around the facts of the past that were hard to blink.

An intimate connection existed between the possession of the sea and possession of these superior qualities. God would have been unlikely to bless an unworthy people with stewardship over the most awesome of His dominions. The English were virtuous, but they were also worthy of their possession because they were naturally born sailors. There seemed to be some confusion over the origin of these seafaring abilities. The notion went all the way back to *Beowulf* in English literature. Some Victorian writers attributed it to the Anglo-Saxon peoples, who "took to the sea like water-dogs" when the brave, wise King Alfred led them forward. Others believed that the English have always been ocean-folk with one fundamental characteristic common to the race: a delight in the sea. The call of the sea was sometimes traced to the ancient Phoenicians, a nation of "ocean-lovers" long before the Greeks and Romans. Although the English were not their direct descendants, they were their spiritual descendants in that "unlike the sailors of other nations, they did not merely cling to the shore, but ventured

29

out into the trackless ocean," an English characteristic and one that was more praiseworthy than the coward's path of hugging the shore.[9]

Some writers thought that nautical daring came from Danish blood, and some traced it back to the Roman influence, although it is unclear whether it was the Romans who brought skill and daring to the island or simply provoked these qualities which had been latent in the resident Britons. One writer claimed that since the Romans came by sea, they must have had some skill and courage with which the natives were in turn infected.[10] Such a conclusion fits in with the rather common association of the late-Victorian empire with its great Roman predecessor.

Whatever the origin of the racial peculiarities, the close association of blood and national policy was an important one. Some histories went as far back as King Alfred for the beginnings of this relationship. Alfred was known to the average Englishman for his revival of learning in the ninth century, for his successful attempts at repelling the Danes, and most of all for establishing the British navy. That great parody of English history, *1066 and All That* (so amusing precisely because of its unerring caricature of the clichés of English schooling) satirized the Alfred story: "Alfred noticed that the Danes had very long ships, so he built a great many, much longer ones, thus cleverly founding the British Navy." A popular *Romance of the Mighty Deep* illustrated these attitudes too, but not facetiously: "King Alfred, of noble memory, coming to the throne, found his country a prey to these marauding Danes. He then and there grasped the principle, which still has sway in England's counsels, that the very existence of Britain as a Nation rests on the strength of her Navy."[11]

The beginning of a definite naval policy, however, was more commonly attributed to the Tudors, who were the first to recognize fully the imperative need to maintain supremacy on the seas with not just a few ships but with an adequate fleet. One writer, whisking through the story of the English navy after Alfred, saw each king as either pro- or anti-navy and accordingly praised or condemned him: Edward III gave the navy much attention; Henry V, though gallant upon land, neglected the navy; Henry VI ignored its claims. The fleet was finally redeemed by the Tudors, especially Henry VIII.[12] Other historians agreed. The conflict between England and Spain during the sixteenth century seemed a good starting point for the association of supremacy with the English racial heritage: "Since Elizabethan times our independence has been secured by our fleet."[13] It is easy to account for such assumptions: sea skill meant sea supremacy; sea supremacy naturally meant a navy; a navy at all worthy of the name was not really in existence before the sixteenth century (King Alfred notwithstanding).

The naval historian J. K. Laughton, in his introduction to a series of naval biographies, thought the matter not so precise. When asked for a date for the beginning of the English navy, he replied that it would be impossible to give one, because "when English history begins, the navy was already an English institution." It is not very clear what he meant, since he failed to define *English*; but he went on to say that very early the Englishmen realized that their security was bound up with the sea. The point he was making, of course, was that shipbuilding was inevitably motivated by love of the sea. He did say, however, that the modern history of the navy might properly be said to begin with the Tudors.[14] Laughton's comment is a particularly significant illustration of the myth of racial possession: if the navy were an institution as old as history, then the relationship of the two would be an ethnic one, predating the social need for defense. We can, therefore, expect to see the use of history to reinforce the one as often as the other.

I spoke of two ways to approach the Victorian sense of the past: in the English self-portrait and in the picture it frames of other peoples. When Victorians looked at the outside world, they perceived it in relation to themselves, much as a child would. This fact points to an important difference between history and mythic history: mythic history is rarely if ever concerned with things, people, and events which do not have direct relevance for its own perception of self. English education in the nineteenth century stressed the classics, and the parallels made at that time between ancient Greece or Rome and the present are instructive.

The greatest empire of the ancient world was Rome; the greatest empire of the modern world was certainly Britain. The temptation to compare the two was irresistible. Britain often came out first in a comparison since she had a number of advantages her predecessor had not, most notable of which was a large and efficient navy to control her dominion "over palm and pine." One naval officer claimed that "no military force in the world's history can point to such a record of almost unbroken victory as the British Navy. This glorious Service holds a position [comparable to that] of Rome." Another important difference between the ancient and modern was Britain's concern with freedom. A newspaper editorial on the occasion of Queen Victoria's second Jubilee Year (1897) commented that the British triumphal procession would differ from the Roman in one important aspect: there were no slaves marching as captured trophies. The British empire, therefore, was more progressive, just, and humane than the Roman. The editorial concluded happily that Britain was "far mightier" than Rome and would endure longer because of her beneficent rule. Lord Cromer, an imperial administrator and expert, found the essential difference between the two in what he called the "spirit" of imperialism. The English spirit was more humane, more civilized, more devoted to the preservation of life ("even useless human life") than the Roman.[15] These attitudes toward empire are important to this study, since the navy was considered both a symbol of empire and an important justification of imperial ambition.

Another deliberate evocation of the Roman past was the term *Pax Britannica*—part fact and part myth in the nineteenth century. Many Englishmen saw the maintenance of Pax Britannica as an inseparable part of the English control of the seas; without the latter you could not have the former. In Christopher Lloyd's admirable short history of the navy, he points out that, while genuine enough in purport, Pax Britannica did not mean a total absence of wars. There were innumerable skirmishes in the hundred years after Napoleon's defeat, but, with the exception of the Crimean War, no major war. Pax Britannica meant, in large part, the use of the navy for diplomatic effect, what was called by some, rather contemptuously, "cruiser diplomacy." But, as Lloyd emphasizes, scorn of nineteenth-century, Palmerstonian policy ignores the fact that similar games are played today: the tools are "situations of strength," but the effect is the same as sending a cruiser to a foreign port or "showing the flag."[16]

Nor were all writers eager to emphasize the naval-military power of British supremacy; one author in a family magazine described the system of International Code of Signals, which had been adopted in 1857 largely on England's initiative, and called it one of the "lasting glories of the Victorian era." He thought the best evidence that Britain was "mistress of the Seas" was not to be found in her Trafalgars but in the fact that she could "give a common language to countless thousands of peoples and nations." This less dramatic work of the navy in the Victorian period was the other side of the Pax Britannica coin, more directly "peaceful," and, to many, just as laudable. Commander Robinson's essay on the British Fleet also stressed the peacetime work of the navy in the nineteenth century: discovery and exploration; charting the seas; the abolition of the slave trade; and the repression of piracy, smuggling, and mutiny—all praiseworthy tasks, indeed—and he summarized these with the comment, "The *Pax Britannica* has replaced the anarchy of the seas."[17]

Although the vision of the imperial giant of the past was an enticing one, I think the comparison of Britain and Rome was never a very comfortable one for English hearts, who did not like to see themselves as conquerors, as slave masters, or as unjust and tyrannical. They warmed instead to the ancient Greeks, particularly to the Athenians, seeing explicit parallels to the situation of Britain. The Greek fight against Persia in the early fifth century B.C. was always pictured as a David-and-Goliath struggle between freedom and tyranny. The historian Sir Charles Oman described how the Asian Greeks begged for aid from the peninsular Greeks against the Persians and finally were able to "throw off the Persian yoke": the giant advances on the helpless democracies; the Athenian leader Themistocles asks the oracle what would save the Greek cities from the Persian hordes and gets the somewhat enigmatic answer, "Trust your wooden walls." Some Athenians argue that this means the fortifications of the Acropolis, but Themistocles says no, wooden walls mean the fleet. He had been responsible for a naval building program and for strengthening the harbor at Piraeus, and some suspected that he simply wanted to prove the worth of his program. But his interpretation carries the day. Accordingly, he orders the evacuation of the city to a place of safety and mobilizes the fleet for combat. The description was typical. Another history stressed that the Athenians were particularly noble because, although they supplied two-thirds of the Greek fleet, they let the Spartans have supreme command at the battle. (The flavor of the nursery dictum Share Your Toys could not be more explicit.)[18]

In the famous battle which ensued in the straits of Salamis, 380 "courageous" little Greek ships faced 1,000 in the Persian fleet. Victorian histories made Salamis a proto-Trafalgar; the ingredients were all there: a fight against heavy odds, unreliable allies, a few cowards who wish to run, a brave commander who rallied the courage of the fleet, a desperate situation finally saved by the superhuman effort and superior virtue of the underdog. When the Greeks saw that the Persian boats were too large and clumsy to maneuver well, they took heart and used their best weapon, the ram, to great advantage. High on the hill overlooking the straits, King Xerxes had built himself a throne from which he could watch the battle. As he sat there through the day he got angrier and angrier and sought a scapegoat. The resemblance to Philip II in 1588 is unmistakable: "From his throne on Aegaleos Xerxes looked down to see his mighty Armada [sic] routed, pursued, and to all intents annihilated by the handful of their antagonists." Like the Spanish king, too, Xerxes decided not to risk another major engagement with the Greek defenders, so he packed up and went home, the defeat having taken "all the spirit out of the barbarians." (Compare this with "Philip must have been very sorry that he began to make war against England.")[19]

The British also pleased themselves that they resembled the ancient Greeks in their public institutions. Victorian histories compared the "democracy" of the past and the present. Walpole thought that the Persians fought because they were whipped, but that the Greeks fought because they were free men, a circumstance that vastly surprised and puzzled the Persian king. Themistocles was portrayed as the patient ruler who knew more and foresaw more than his fellow Greeks. He luckily had the authority and the conviction to insist on his naval building program, and he was wise enough to see where and how the battle had to be fought. Themistocles achieved greatness not because he was a tyrant with overweening power, however, but because he was the wise leader of free men. He saw the need to make Athens a sea power and the wisdom of sacrificing an army to a navy.[20]

❀　　❀　　❀

This discussion of the Victorian view of the classical past indicates how very biased (by our present standards) was the Victorian approach to history. The ancient world suffered from this historicism more than other times for two reasons: first, English education placed greater emphasis upon the classics in the Victorian period; and, second, the more distant the historical period the more susceptible it was to manipulation for mythic purposes. But to a great extent, the mythologizing affected other historical periods as well. When the Victorians looked at the more recent past they saw nothing to disturb their "Whiggish" vision that history was a long, glorious sweep upwards. With respect to Britain and the sea, the sweep seemed to start in the sixteenth century. The greatness of the English seaman dated fairly specifically in the English mind from the piratical buccaneers of Elizabethan times and was re-echoed in the naval heroes like Admiral Blake of the seventeenth and early eighteenth centuries. As the skill of the seaman grew, so grew the strength and grandeur of the navy, and it took on an aura of sanctity in this period. The eighteenth century was seen as the era of the "second hundred years war"—a long conflict with France that ended, quite predictably, in France's defeat and in the downfall of the tyrant Napoleon.

Thus began the period when the Romantic revival of the past (particularly of Greek history and folk cultures) fed into and enlarged the mythic import of history. This was also the period when Britain began to play the leading part on the world stage, and she became conscious of her great resources, her mighty sea power, and the importance of her role. According to the myth, though, it was well after the death of Nelson in 1805 that Britain came to a full realization of her responsibilities.[21]

An anonymous naval peer illustrated this realization in a book, *Our Naval Position*, in which he claimed that British sailors had built their renown on the subjugation of three first-rate navies (those of Spain, Holland, and France in historical order) and upon having swept every hostile flag from the ocean: "in short, by making every sea tributary, every island held by an enemy a spoil, and planting the flag of England on the four quarters of the globe, from the rising to the setting sun." A schoolbook of the Edwardian era also emphasized that Great Britain in the nineteenth century had a monopoly of the world's commerce because of her superior command of the sea, which in turn increased trade. The reason for such command was that the United States was too young to compete, China and Japan were "asleep," and "various nations of Europe were always fighting or preparing to fight." The moral was that if you attend to your own business, stay out of Europe's troubles, and look to your boats, you will get ahead and be "free, rich and quiet," to use Lord Halifax's words of 1694. Britain could do this; other countries could not.[22]

We see these attitudes toward other countries very clearly in some of the slogans of the nineteenth century, probably the most famous of which was Rule Britannica, dating from an eighteenth-century song written by James Thomson. The song is worth quoting here because it illustrates some of the myths that we have been discussing: Britain's special niche in God's love; her role as super-guardian of the sea; and her special reward, a freedom from tyranny, which other nations may envy but would not achieve.

Rule Britannia

When Britain first, at Heaven's command,
Arose from out the azure main,
This was the charter of her land,
And guardian angels sung the strain:
    Rule, Britannia! Rule the waves!
    Britons never will be slaves!

The nations not so blest as thee,
Must in their turn to tyrants fall;
Whilst thou shalt flourish, great and free,
The dread and envy of them all.
    [repeat refrain][23]

The association of Rule Britannia with naval supremacy (Rule Britannia and Mistress of the Seas were very frequently linked in popular parlance) is caricatured in *1066 and All That*: "From that time onwards foreigners who, unlike the English, do not prefer to fight against long odds, seldom attacked the British Navy. Hence the important International law called Rule Britannia, technically known as Freedom of the Seas." But in the Victorian period it was more usual to take the phrase seriously than to be amused by it. In 1896 the earl of Malmesbury in a talk, "The Navy in the House of Lords," called the phrase Rule Britannia "the summing-up, in fact, within poetic limits, of a Heaven-sent message, proclaiming for our race the Sovereignty of the Seas."[24]

Such boasting illustrates a kind of Victorian morality and self-righteousness which both intrigued and infuriated non-British peoples. It was implicit in one of the Navy League pamphlets in which the sailor was described as the policeman of the pathless sea and which claimed that England's command of the seas had come to her because of her superior virtue: she was "mistress of the seas" not for her own glory, but in order that she might hold the ocean for the "preservation of peace and civilisation." Such a task would be very pleasing to God, and, in his turn, the sailor would not let God down but be steadfast in his path of duty.[25]

When Tennyson wrote of the empire,

One with Britain, heart and soul!
One life, one flag, one fleet, one throne!
Britons, hold your own![26]

he simply phrased the imperial and worldwide contemporary mission as seen by the Victorian moralists and historians. The smugness of racial superiority is offensive—as is all smugness—but it would be hard to term it accurately hypocritical. These late-Victorian notions of duty, of mission for the oppressed (that is, the rest of the world), and of the fleet which rightfully possessed the seas were certainly sincere. We must not confuse understanding with approval.

The nineteenth century saw the full fruition of the sea-myth with its attendant attitudes and slogans. As Britain looked at her history, as she compared herself with past and present, her pride of place seemed assured.

4

The Myths of Islandhood

We are an island, we are confined to it by God Almighty, not as a penalty but a grace, and one of the greatest that can be given to mankind. Happy confinement, that hath made us free, rich, and quiet; a fair portion in this world, and very well worth the preserving; a figure that ever hath been envied, and could never be imitated by our neighbours.

Marquis of Halifax, 1694

THE RELATIONSHIP BETWEEN THE ISLAND AND THE SURROUNDING SEA is an intimate one. Not only does the sea literally define the island, it also poses for the islander the danger and challenge which dares him to venture forth, both literally and metaphorically. As the sea encloses the island so the islander must come to terms with his surroundings and prove himself on the sea as the warrior does on the land.

Shakespeare called England "this sceptr'd isle/This precious stone set in a silver sea," and Dryden, "Fairest isle, all isles excelling." It would be hard to overestimate the important psychology of separateness which has arisen as a result of the geographical accident of the English Channel, dividing by a mere twenty-odd miles the coast of England from the mainland of Europe. Were it not for this accident, I think, the sea-mythology might have been significantly different from what it was. Because these feelings of separateness are so bound up with the English mystique and self-image, it seems appropriate to examine in some detail the myth of island existence in connection with the mythology of the sea.

The Marquis of Halifax's words "happy confinement" convey the image of the island as oasis. This is quite an ancient idea, dating back to classical times. The oasis or heaven (Shakespeare: "this other Eden, demi-paradise") represents security, refreshment, reward, and safety, set off as it is from the rest of the world by a

38

definable barrier, quarantined from contamination by the sick and evil of the world. The island is surrounded by the asceptic and purifying sea. The garden image is important also because the primary characteristic in Eden was innocence, that is, not evil overcome but pre-evil; a place where, as W. H. Auden puts it, "there is no conflict between natural desire and moral duty."[1] The comment is significant, I think, because in the Victorian ideal there *was* no necessary conflict; in fact ideally one would speak of natural desire and moral duty not as two but as one. To the extent that man falls away from God, the first becomes separated from the second, and the second is forgotten. One can certainly find (in Kingsley, say, or George Eliot) the struggle to make the two synonymous. And as one is quarantined from the evil of the world—confined to the island not as a penalty but as a grace—one is given an opportunity to pursue the moral duty with a head start on other peoples. Islandhood, therefore, becomes a privileged position but imposes (as does all privilege, the Victorians thought) special responsibilities which might be more arduous than those given to lesser folk.

The island metaphor is, of course, very old. One is reminded of Bacon, of Shakespeare, or the prototypal *Utopia* of Sir Thomas More, as well as the more modern Defoe or Stevenson. Sometimes the island figures as refuge, sometimes as temptation; it can represent innocence or evil, freedom or slavery, paradise or purgatory. It bears this symbolic burden precisely because by its very nature it is separate from ordinary life. There is an interesting example of island imagery in Tennyson's "Voyage of Maeldune," a poem based loosely on an eighth-century Irish legend. Maeldune sets out to avenge the death of his father and lands at nine different islands, each associated with a different danger, each offering temptations, all of which eventually decimate his crew. Finally Maeldune finds his father's slayer, but he has learned that vengeance brings only unhappiness and further suffering. The islands are both "devilish" (in that they are a source of evil) and "divine" (in that they are the means by which man is taught virtue). The island as a mechanism for the testing of man need not be sacred; it could as easily be secular. *Robinson Crusoe* comes to mind, or *Treasure Island* or *The Admirable Crichton* or the contemporary *Lord of the Flies.*

As islandhood conveys special status upon the islander, it also affords him security. The island is physically as well as morally and metaphorically separate, and thus represents safety. As one shuts out evil, one shuts out also the danger from those who are envious, wanton invaders of one's privacy. I shall consider in this chapter these twin myths: the special status of the islander and his physical security from invasion.

In 1882, the historian E. A. Freeman wrote an article for the *Contemporary Review* entitled "Alter Orbis" ("Other World"). The ideas expressed in this article were so characteristic of this view of the national self—Britain as a different world—that it bears examination. Freeman identified as one of the most important parts of the British national mentality what he called its "insular" character. He felt that island existence imparted, in a very real sense, a special habit of mind that could not be found elsewhere. To that insular character Freeman attributed a racial quality which the English supposedly took with them wherever they went throughout the world. Thus he argued that the dependent colonists of Great Britain were somehow "islanders" even when they did not dwell on islands.[2]

Islandhood to Freeman meant a distinctive spirit of nautical adventure, and since island races were considered to be superior to the common folk of the rest of the world, they were set apart racially as well as geographically. He even allowed the people of the United States into the select club of "islanders," attributing a large portion of their distinctive character to the English influence on American history. (By 1882, of course, America's melting pot was surely bubbling away, and the infusion of nonislanders must have been very large, statistically, but Freeman ignored this fact.) Thus for him the term *islanders* very conveniently meant both those who were directly related by blood to the English and those peoples of whom he approved—an exact as well as a metaphorical or symbolic meaning. With some complacency he wrote, "Some may wish, perhaps, the character of the English folk in either hemisphere to be other than it is, and doubtless we are not so perfect in either hemisphere that we could not stand some improvement," but this is a mere sop to the canons of taste and humility; nowhere in the article is there evidence that he thought much improvement was needed.[3]

Islandhood is, of course, a characteristic which other seafaring nationalities share with Britain. Freeman made it clear that some of the greatness of being insular had rubbed off on others. The history of Venice, for example, would have been significantly different had she been part of the mainland of Italy, and similarly the history of the Greek islands, of Sicily, Ireland, and other places throughout the world. Nevertheless, however much their geographic position had affected their history, none of them could quite aspire to the wholly independent rank of *alter orbis*. Each had to be content to depend on a larger system. Only Britain could boast the single rank of *alter orbis*: "It is Britain alone that has been truly deemed another world from the very beginning of her known being."[4]

Freeman traced the fortunes of this British island from Roman times to the present, showing how at every stage in her history Britain's surrounding sea made a significant and frequently overwhelming contribution to the outcome of events. As he put it very strongly in another essay:

> Our insular position has been one of the greatest facts of our history; it has caused a distinction between us islanders and our neighbours on the Continent which is independent of all distinctions of race, language, or religion, and which is often found at cross-purposes with all of them. We feel at once that there are some points, great and small, in which we stand by ourselves in opposition to continentals, simply as continentals. This is a fact which should carefully be borne in mind, because some points of difference between ourselves and our kinfolk on the mainland, which are really owing simply to our geographical isolation, have been set down as proofs of imaginary Roman or British influences in England.[5]

Freeman conceded that, racially speaking, the inhabitants of Britain were Celtic and Teutonic, that Celts and Teutons lived in Europe as well, and that in fact the English were racially very closely akin to their neighbors across the Channel. However, as the quotation makes clear, an intangible but very significant difference existed between these island people and the continentals, a difference that far outweighed any superficial likeness. If one aspired to a rank of greatness, therefore, it would help to live on an island; but one would never be in the ranks of the truly great unless one were British by birth, by genealogical descent, or possibly by "spiritual" descent.[6]

Freeman described Britain as from the beginning a nation of fiercely independent, strong (but not tyrannical) peoples, independent of viewpoint and jealous of their isolation. His description of the Roman conquest had Caesar facing "stout resistance" from the ancient Britons, a very nationalistic people even in defeat. When the Romans withdrew, "a nation sprang to life again, a nation which still abides. That Britain still contains a British people, speaking a British tongue, is one of the results of the ruling fact that

41

Britain is an island."[7] This "ruling fact" is interesting to us not so much for its historical accuracy (it would be pretty hard to document) but for its mythic effect. According to Freeman, the enveloping ocean that had made a Briton British in Caesar's time still made an Englishman English in modern times. Englishmen remained "pure" in race and attitude as opposed to other peoples who were, perforce, mixed and combined.

The purity of the English blood came not only from isolation, however, but from a domination over other nations and races. Britain's vulnerability to invasion from the sixth to the eleventh centuries suggested to Freeman the magnetlike quality that Britain had for other peoples who recognized the desirability of Britain and the British and thus wanted to possess the island. When the land had absorbed these invading peoples, it quickly made them its own; they were integrated into a national personality, totally submerged in the superior blood, with no traces of their former selves.[8] In another essay, Freeman made a similar point, arguing that by the time of Henry III in the thirteenth century, the Norman invader had "drunk in the air of the free island, and had learned that the laws of Good King Edward were as good for him as for his English neighbour," and so he speedily adopted the feelings, the name, and at last the language of Englishmen.[9] Thus Roman, Saxon, Angle, Jute, Dane, and finally Norman crossed the seas, conquered, and then succumbed to the joys of being English (or perhaps British), adding their own strengths—but not their weaknesses—to the blood of the islander and being, in turn, the object of malice and jealousy from abroad.

Lest it be thought that these were just the vagaries of a somewhat unreliable historian, I cite the memoir of Ford Madox Ford, which also reflects this view of mythic history. In a discussion of race and the English spirit, he remarked that he and his schoolfellows thought of the Normans as being "English" because "they were the first to show the true genius of the race"! And, further, that

> In our history, as we had confronted its spirit, a touch of English soil was sufficient to do as much for William the Norman, who, though we call him a Conqueror, seems to most English boys eminently more English than the Anglo-Saxon [Harold] who was weak enough to get shot in the eye. Similarly, for the English boy, the Plantagenets, the Tudors, the Scotch Stuarts, the Hanoverian Guelphs, and even Dutch William—all these kings became "English" the moment they ruled in England.[10]

Thus the isolation of islandhood confers a "nationality" upon an alien race, while it preserves a separate identity for the islanders.

Isolated as Britain was—or felt herself to be—it was inevitable that she make a virtue out of being uninvolved in Continental politics, a policy known as *splendid isolation* in the late-Victorian era. When she chose to interfere (as she sometimes did), she felt able to act from purely disinterested motives. The purifying sea gave her a moral strength which other nations unfortunately lacked. We find the idea that isolation gave strength phrased differently, but with no less conviction, by some of the other writers of the same period. Commander Charles N. Robinson attributed British freedom to the fact of her separate existence as an island: "Our insularity, in short, made potential by our fleets, has given us freedom from the burdens that weigh upon others." There were, however, possible dangers to insularity: Englishmen might become complacent and too apathetic to face the challenges of another's envy. Frederick Greenwood, an essayist and editor, was so alarmed at this possibility in 1895 that he urged Englishmen who were shut up within their island security to be vigilant for possible trouble in Far East or West. He wondered if the long peace that England had enjoyed would not work to her disadvantage in that it might have softened her, weakened her vision, and made her easy prey to envious wolves.[11]

An editorial in the *Monthly Review* a few years later discussed England's unpopularity with other nations, particularly European nations, and tried to account for it in the following way: all peoples hate foreigners, but on the Continent, where you live so close to your neighbors, you must be tactful and tolerant of them, or at least quiet about their shortcomings. This was not true with England, which lay protected and separate; therefore, the neighbors could criticize her without fear of punishment. Not only was it safe to criticize and hate her, it was very natural: "We are Islanders. We are stranger, more foreign than other foreigners."[12] The complacent, almost paranoid idea that everyone hated and envied Britain may have had some foundation in historical fact, but what is interesting was the easy assumption of its truth. Indeed, Britain seemed to take a kind of perverse pride in such hatred. Englishmen assumed that they were envied not only for their riches but also for their superior institutions, their freedom, their parliamentary government, and their relative domestic peace. As one writer put it, "We are what we are because of our glorious inheritance of valor, self-reliance, and of liberty brought by our ancestors from over sea."[13]

It was not simply mere common patriotism that led the English to boast of their institutions, as any country might. The Englishman was impressed with the self-evident facts of British greatness; the Pax Britannica, undoubted civil freedom in England, and the lack of a standing army and its expense all seemed such unquestionable virtues in political life that it was inconceivable that they would not be desired by every other rational nation. "Our law and system of government are alike different from those of the rest of Europe." Nowhere was the idea of equality before the law understood as it was in the British Empire and the United States.[14]

There seems to be some validity in the historical judgment that because England *felt* herself separate, whatever the facts of the slimness of her geographical isolation, she tended to look outward from her position and away from Continental quarrels. Thus her "splendid isolation" may have accounted, at least in part, for her interest in empire, when by preference the adventurous spirit turned to maritime explorations rather than to military glory in Continental battles. Whatever its basis in reality, this belief became a frequently expressed cliché of the nation's history. The editor of a popular anthology of sea poetry thought that because Britain was the only large and fruitful island of the Old World, she was naturally the "child of the sea" (island existence being equated with nautical skill). It was then inevitable "that the high road of the ocean should lead [the Englishman] all over the world." Hence England's destiny as "the august mother of empires."[15] The editor goes on to warn, however, that this superiority of history and of skill should not give rise to vainglory in the Englishman's breast but rather should make him modest and humble before such vast responsibilities.

We find a similar attitude throughout Rudyard Kipling's poetry. One poem, written in 1902, significantly titled "The Islanders," has these particular lines:

> No doubt but ye are the People—your throne
> is above the King's
>
> . . . .
>
> Fenced by your careful fathers, ringed by
> your leaden seas

Kipling exhorted the British to work harder, to be worthy of the divine mandate for service, cautioning that superiority in strength,

44

in virtue, and in institutions must breed not indolence but a greater dedication to the responsibility of helping the unfortunate:

> No doubt but ye are the People—absolute, strong,
>   and wise;
> Whatever your heart has desired ye have not withheld
>   from your eyes.
> On your own heads, in your own hands, the sin and
>   the saving lies!

Claims to exclusiveness are evident, perhaps, in all national patriotic poetry, but because Britain seemed to have both geographic excuse and historical justification for aloofness (the argument was buttressed with much pseudoscientific data) there is a peculiarly compelling quality about such expressions.

Confinement on an island may have made Britain "free, rich, and quiet," as Halifax supposed, but there was, after all, a very narrow sleeve of water separating England from the Continent. The fears that arise when that confinement is threatened by the proposed Channel tunnel are instructive.[16]

＊　　＊　　＊

In 1870, Gladstone published anonymously an article in the *Edinburgh Review* analyzing England's relationship to Continental politics. Eloquent on the need for isolation, he dwelt for a few paragraphs on the happy accident of the existence of the English Channel. He called it the "wise dispensation of Providence" and "that streak of silver sea" (a partial reference to Shakespeare's image) thus perhaps inadvertently coining a phrase that was to have great currency for the next forty years. The Silver Streak became a common nickname for the English Channel with its providential ability to protect, isolate, and keep pure the English sensibility. Gladstone was not alone in attributing the Silver Streak to the hand of God. Many seemed to feel that God had been especially kind to Britain in giving her this narrow channel to set her off by an almost impassable barrier from the lesser people to the East. But, as with all divine gifts, there was a condition. Gladstone wrote, "Where the Almighty grants exceptional and peculiar bounties, He sometimes permits by way of counterpoise an insensibility to their value. Were there but a slight upward heaving of the crust of the earth between France and Great Britain, and were dry land thus to be substituted for a few leagues of sea, then indeed we should begin to know what we had lost."[17] Luckily, there seemed no chance that God would be so unkind as to heave up the crust.

Alfred Austin (later to be poet laureate after Tennyson's death), upon returning to Britain in 1882, wrote three sonnets on the English Channel that reflect this half-conscious feeling of the providential nature of England's position. The third poem starts this way:

> And can it be, when Heaven this deep moat made,
> And filled it with the ungovernable seas,
> Gave us the winds for rampart, waves for frise,
> Behind which freedom, elsewhere if betrayed,
> Might shelter find, and flourish unafraid.

The question the poem asks recalls an important Victorian theme: if England were to forget her mission, her special role and responsibilities, if she were to lie about, pampering herself with "womanish ease," might she not deservedly perish in a grave of gold?[18]

Naval writers also stressed the divine purpose of this "deep moat." Robinson and Leyland, in their book *For the Honour of the Flag*, believed that the role of the Channel was "to preserve this England of ours, hedged in with the main, that water-walled bulwark, secure and confident from foreign purposes."[19] As is implicit in their comment, the function of the Silver Streak was two-fold: partly it protected England—again and again the Channel is referred to as a "barrier" or "bulwark" against the depredations of foreigners—but it also served as a symbolic representation of the elite quality of England herself. How much more difficult it would have been, for example, to think of oneself as separate when sharing a common frontier with another country not de-limited by any dramatic geographical feature or outline, such as a body of water. It was, after all, the Channel that made Britain an island.

For a relatively small piece of water (only twenty-one miles wide at its narrowest), the English Channel is extraordinarily rough and unpleasant. Storms and high seas are the rule rather than the exception. The channel is narrow and shallow: at its narrowest part, it is never more than 216 feet deep, and for half of the distance across, it is under 100 feet deep. The combination of narrowness, depth, and the strong winds flowing through the neck of the Channel made almost any crossing formidable. English travelers frequently wrote home of the horrors of the trip. W. S. Gilbert's Lord Chancellor in *Iolanthe* describes his nightmare to "dream you are crossing/the Channel and tossing/about in a steamer from Harwich," and another writer claimed, "Probably there is no other piece of traveling in civilized countries where, within equal times, so much suffering is endured; certainly it would be hard to find another voyage of equal length which is so much feared." An amusing contemporary cartoon showed a parliamentary wife on the deck of a Channel steamer, obviously suffering from seasickness, exclaiming as she leans against her husband's shoulder, "Oh! William dear—if you are—a Liberal—do bring in a Bill—next Session —for that Underground Tunnel!"[20]

But for all their misery with seasickness, the British took a kind of perverse pride in the horrors of the crossing. Some seemed to think the difficulty a direct sign from the Almighty that the Channel was not to be considered in the same class as other bodies of water, nor were such journeys to be undertaken lightly. The notion that England's bad weather in the Channel and on land was a divine favor illustrates a peculiar Victorian habit of seeing a weakness as a strength, black as white, calamity as good fortune. Austin's first sonnet talks of going home from "climes that fancy deems more fair." He knows that when he gets to England there will no soft foam on the smiling strand, no orange groves, no mild zephyrs, only "Amazonian March" with sleet and wind and horrid weather. And yet, he blesses the "brave, bleak land" where he was born, since he feels that, after all, there is something a little suspect about "sensuous slopes that bask 'neath Southern skies." (For the earnest Victorian, to be sensuous was tantamount to forgetting God and one's duty.)[21]

According to the dogma, the channel was Britain's major defense against that ultimate of horrors, invasion. As one anthologist wrote, "Thanks to the 'silver streak' which is worth an entire European army, the English race, instead of exhausting its force, as the other less lucky races have been obliged to do, in defending frontiers, has been enabled to give all its energies to strengthening its limbs at home and finding fresh fields in which to exercise them abroad."[22] This fear of invasion was very real but probably not very rational. The English myth proudly supposed that ever since William the Norman in 1066 no one had successfully invaded England, conveniently forgetting Monmouth and William of Orange in the seventeenth century, to say nothing of the Jacobite troubles in the eighteenth century, among others. If taxed with

47

these examples, the Englishman would be apt to say there had been no successful "foreign" invasion, since William III was married to an Englishwoman, Monmouth was English, and the Stuarts British, or at least Scottish.

It all depended upon one's definitions of *foreign* and *invasion*, but it will not do simply to scoff at the clumsiness of the language, since what is important is the very real quality of the fear itself, according to which all foreigners would have liked nothing better than to make the dread crossing of the English Channel and subdue the English people. By defining certain incursions as non-invasions, the myth functioned to help keep that fear at bay. An interesting short story in *Pearson's Magazine* called "Where Will the Enemy Land?" illustrates this fear in a different way. An unnamed enemy lands at Harwich, where the troops cut the telegraph wires, take the train to Colchester, seize the station and then the barracks, and attempt to terrorize the population. The speculation on the possible landing sites is interesting: the author concluded that the Norfolk coast would be particularly good because it would be deserted and undefended. He also suggested the possibility of an invasion in the Wash and at King's Lynn. The secrets of the enemy's success were, first, surprise; second, knowledge of English geography; and third, the use of a fifth column of foreign nationals resident in England.[23]

The story was like a child's ghost story: it had a pleasingly scary quality behind the make-believe (the enemy showed no mercy: "brutality calculated to strike terror in every heart"), but it had the same fictional flavor that every good ghost story has: when the child is scared he can always reach for Nurse's knee and reassure himself that it is, after all, just a story. The moral of the tale was that Britain should have a "real army," trained and disciplined, and an adequate navy. These were not terribly original ideas, certainly, but rather amusingly and differently expressed in this well-told story. (In an accompanying illustration the foreign soldiers look very fierce and uncompromising; the English properly alarmed.) Another fictional treatment of the same theme, *The Riddle of the Sands*, by Erskine Childers, was published at the turn of the century. In this novel, Germany is explicitly the enemy, and the mystery hinges on the discovery of an invasion fleet hidden in the tidewater flats of the Friesian islands.

The fear of invasion was not limited to writers of fiction; it was a common public alarm. Commander Robinson in a picture book for children attributed to King Alfred the first recognition of the need to be prepared against invasion and claimed that Alfred was the first one in English history to recognize that to wait for the enemy to land was "to give them half the victory." No doubt this is sound advice, but it also demonstrates the fearful withdrawal that we saw in the need to feel surrounded by the sea—a kind of unconscious pushing away of danger to a neutral distance. For a long time the Channel filled this role of the moat that keeps danger at arm's length, but there came a change late in the century when it no longer seemed so powerful a protector. As early as 1859 a naval peer (not otherwise identified), who was worried about a possible French invasion, thought that with the advent of a steam navy the English Channel was not the barrier it had been but had now become in some senses a "bridge" to England. He was alarmed enough to urge a naval force superior to any other possible combination of enemy fleets.[24] But he was very much ahead of his time; the real invasion scares came a good twenty or thirty years later.

A modern historian remarks that the Channel was more than a geographical fact, it was a state of mind.[25] It has been this state of mind, this clinging to the myth of separation, that has defeated every attempt to bridge the gap. Over the past two centuries several proposals have been advanced to construct either a tunnel or a bridge across the Channel. These proposals (which were all unsuccessful) are instructive in illustrating how important the separateness has been.

As early as 1802 a scheme for a tunnel was proposed in France by a mining engineer. In 1833 the subject came up again, the earlier proposal having come to nought. It also failed, and in the 1840s and 1850s various explorations of the Channel were made (mostly by French engineers) to determine the feasibility of putting a tunnel through the rock formations under the straits. The idea had a mixed reception in England: Prince Albert supported the idea, apparently with enthusiasm, and persuaded the queen that there might be distinct advantages for those who were prone to seasicknesses (as she was). Certainly a tunnel that would smoothly convey travelers to the Continent would eliminate a major barrier to the comforts of travel, but there were many in high places who felt the benefits would not outweigh the disadvantages. On one occasion a French tunnel engineer was talking to Lord Palmerston in an interview at which Prince Albert was present. Palmerston was not in favor of the tunnel, and, according to the engineer, when the prince consort spoke of the benefits to England, Lord Palmerston "without losing that perfectly courteous tone that was habitual

49

with him," told Prince Albert that His Highness would feel quite differently had he "been born on this island." He thus neatly rubbed in the fact that the British had never quite accepted the prince.[26]

Events in France during the reign of Napoleon III brought about a wave of invasion fears, and the tunnel project was dropped for some ten years. The great engineering success of the Suez Canal led to renewed efforts to promote a tunnel, and in 1870 a group of French investors persuaded their government to ask the British government for support of a joint scheme. The Franco-Prussian War intervened and the project was again shelved. In 1872 the French government made inquiries once more, and after a long delay the British government replied that it had no objection "in principle" to a tunnel, provided that it would be under private ownership and construction; public money would not be spent on such a visionary scheme. This effectively scotched the idea.

In 1882 came the first full-scale attempt to promote and construct a sub-Channel tunnel from near Dover to France. The attempt was directed by an enterprising man named Sir Edward Watkins, who spent a great deal of time and money, and who might even have succeeded had it not been for the storm of controversy that arose over the project, apparently caused in part by an article in the *Times* in June of 1881. The debate was carried on in the pages of the press and the reviews. Basically the question raised was, If a tunnel were constructed, would England be more vulnerable to an invasion? The *Times* feared that a force of several thousand men could be suddenly landed on the Kentish coast and surprise the English at their own end of the tunnel.[27]

Lord Dunsany, a naval officer, opened a long debate in the columns of *Nineteenth Century* with an article called "The Silver Streak," in which he expressed extreme concern at the prospect, indeed, the real possibility, of invasion via tunnel. The following year, in the February issue, he wrote another article, "The Proposed Channel Tunnel," which was even more hysterical in tone. Colonel Frederick Beaumont, an engineer and architect involved in the tunnel scheme; Goldwin Smith, historian and essayist; and John Fowler, a barrister; took up the cudgels to reply to or support Dunsany the following month. Lord Brabourne, a Liberal M.P., also entered the lists with an article in *Contemporary Review*. The two sides rarely listened to each other, although they made pretense of answering each others' arguments.[28]

The opponents of the tunnel were alarmed at the thought of a French army marching through (a three-hour journey, as one military writer estimated) in the dead of night, surprising the Dover garrison and effecting a dramatic and quick defeat the following morning. It was, indeed, a hideous and unthinkable notion. Lord Dunsany thought it was feasible. As a professional navy man he perhaps had special knowledge, though he seemed to bring no particular expertise to the subject and used as his authority the famous and respected army officer, Sir Garnet (later Lord) Wolseley, known for his imperial service and rigid authoritarianism. Wolseley was unalterably opposed to the idea of the tunnel.

Its supporters argued that the tunnel would actually be a very poor avenue for invasion since at the English end it could be blown up, gassed, flooded, or otherwise made inoperable in a matter of a few minutes. No nation would risk entombing a division of soldiers on the remote chance of capturing the fort at Dover. Brabourne quoted an unnamed admiral as saying with heavy sarcasm, "The navy of England has guarded the whole extent of her shores for some few hundreds of years past, and it is odd if we cannot trust the army of England to guard the mouth of one little hole." (A double thrust here, since some of the public were, in fact, that dubious of the army's ability.) Brabourne went on to wonder if an army officer would not be delighted to have his enemy's invading soldiers so nicely contained that they would have to advance through a very narrow outlet. He suggested that the unprotected harbors of the North Sea coast were a much greater temptation to a foe than any tunnel. After all, to supply an invasion force adequately an enemy would need control of the Channel anyway, and if he had that he would not need the tunnel. Any enemy would be idiotic to want to land at Dover, with the castle and fortifications frowning from the heights. Finally, Brabourne charged that all of Dunsany's and Wolseley's fears were based on the unsound notion that England would have to be completely changed in her nature, habit, and feeling: she would have to be stupid, blind, unsuspicious, and incompetent to be taken by surprise in such a fashion.[29]

Other supporters of the tunnel agreed with Lord Brabourne, and worried that Britain was beginning to look a little ridiculous in the world's eyes. An article in the *Standard*, quoting its Berlin correspondent, summarized the German view of the tunnel in the words of Count Moltke, who thought it a very progressive idea. He dismissed any notion of a tunnel invasion of England as suicidal, because commonsensical precautions could so easily defeat the invader. The Germans were disposed to poke a little fun at what they considered absurd English alarm. The *Manchester Guardian* sided with the Germans; a few heavy guns at the mouth of the tunnel would take care of any danger.[30]

The proponents of the tunnel felt that England would have a great deal to gain from its construction: not only the removal of a difficult journey, but also the increase of commerce and the consequent improvement of economic and international relations. The *Pall Mall Gazette* published an anonymous letter on the advantages of the tunnel: it would bring more tourists to England (a "pacific invasion" the writer called it), and it would mean greater friendship between England and France. The *Daily News* objected to the "illiberality" of the arguments against the tunnel. Its writer thought it would promote greater freedom of communication between nations and encourage English prosperity—all worthy aims and ones which every forward-looking Englishman of the modern period ought to support.[31]

An opposing argument, curiously circular, was expressed in a letter to the *Times*. A tunnel would naturally take "goods traffic" and therefore would mean an inevitable decline in the mercantile marine which presently transported those goods. Thus, by extension, the seaports dependent upon that trade would also decline. England would therefore become a second-rate power. A very gloomy conclusion and one which illustrates the force of the myth: sea supremacy was a given principle.[32]

An index of how strong these fears were may be seen in a public protest that appeared in the April 1882 issue of *Nineteenth Century*. It was signed by 54 notables: M.P.'s, barristers, journalists, including Tennyson, Browning, and Cardinal Manning. The editor of the journal suggested that those who agreed with the petition should write in and add their names. The following month, *Nineteenth Century* published an impressive list with well over 500 more names; including churchmen, peers, and politicians as well as scores of army and naval officers.

The pro-and-con arguments over the tunnel project were emotional, even hysterical, rather than rational. Indeed, what reasonable objections the opponents raised were always well answered by the supporters. But, in the end the government withdrew its minimal support, and the project failed, not to be broached again for another twenty or thirty years. Provided that the problems of engineering and finance could be solved, it seems in retrospect that a tunnel would have been of benefit to Britain. It was probably impossible to construct it with private capital; it would have had to have been a government project, and no government was going to risk its life on such a politically dangerous idea. Enough of the public apparently agreed with a letter to the *Standard* from "A Traveller": France with vast armies had everything to gain from a tunnel and nothing to lose, but England stood to lose "the integrity of her seaboard" and to gain very little. Until some solid national advantage could be demonstrated, the writer said, let us go on suffering seasickness rather than suffer a national calamity.[33]

❀   ❀   ❀

The details of this particular occasion of the tunnel controversy illustrate the intensity of the myths of islandhood, cloaked as they might have been in pseudorational arguments. Britain was willing to suffer the ridicule of continentals, to allow many stockholders to go broke, and to break the spirit and the health of an intensely committed and capable person (Watkins) in order that she be allowed to forget this notion, this terrible and devilish scheme to join her firmly to a European continent that she would rather not join. The present-day situation with the Common Market illustrates how the wheel has come full circle: Britain's destiny and future health now seem to be inextricably bound up with Europe's, but many of the arguments against her joining the market were markedly reminiscent of those used in the 1880s: her need to feel free of continental entanglements, her need, basically, to feel separate.

Probably the best expression of this need comes from Freeman's article (parts of which I have quoted earlier). He wrote, "We are islanders: and I at least do not wish that we should become continentals. My only reason for being set against the tunnel is a fear— perhaps not altogether a fear, rather a mere vague kind of feeling —that it may do something, in sentiment at least, towards making us cease to be islanders and become continentals." And most people were disposed to agree with the *Times* when it concluded, "Nature is on our side at present and she will continue so if we will only suffer [allow] her. The Silver Streak is our safety."[34]

It might have been a "vague feeling," but it was a real one— and of such is myth made. To be joined to the Continent was to become continental. Englishmen did *not* want to become continentals in sentiment or in any other way; they cherished their islandhood. The sea provided their uniqueness and their safety. Any attempt to bridge the God-given gap of the Channel was not to be borne.

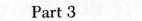

Part 3

THE MYTHS OF SEAMANSHIP

THIS SECTION CONCERNS THE MOST INDIVIDUAL ELEMENT IN THE VIC-
torian myth of the sea: the "tar who ploughed the waters," who
manned the ships of the navy. Chapter 5 deals with the sometimes confused image of the seaman, with his qualities and his
training. Chapter 6 concerns the myth of the Armada, an event in
the English past which had assumed mythic proportions as the
birthplace of English seamanship. Finally, Chapter 7 deals with
the ultimate naval hero, Lord Nelson, who embodied for the Victorians so much of what they believed about themselves, and who
in large measure personified the sea myth.

5

The English Seaman

"It is not for us to mind State matters, but to keep foreigners from fooling us"—that has been the motto of the Naval profession, and probably no profession has inspired such disinterested affection or bred such a race of simple heroes.

Q, *Story of the Sea*

Did a British heart quail? Not one. To do or die was luminously written on every resolute face.

"True British," in *Comrades*

The dark blue jacket that enfolds the sailor's manly breast
Bears more of real honour than the star and ermine crest.

Eliza Cook

IF THE ENGLISH ASSUMED THAT THE SEA BELONGED TO THEM BY divine inheritance, it is scarcely surprising that they should also assume that they had some special racial skill with ships, some inborn nautical virtue. The historian E. A. Freeman once wrote, "We came by sea, by no other way indeed could we make our way to an island. But we came by sea in another sense from that in which Roman Caesar came by sea and Norman William came after him. We came by sea not simply because the sea was the only road, but because we came as folk of the sea to whom the sea was not a mere path but a true home." J. A. Froude expressed a similar idea: "After their island the sea is the natural home of the English man; the Norse blood is in us, and we rove over the waters, for business or pleasure, as eagerly as our ancestors." If the sea were "home," it was natural, then, to endow the sailor with those qualities considered especially English, admirable in those of "Norse blood."[1]

57

The presumption that the sailor was a kind of national distillation was common. Professor Laughton, the naval historian, believed that "sailors differ from their countrymen mainly in being finer specimens of the race." Sometimes the sailor is a personification of virtue, sometimes just a very reliable fellow: "Whenever I want a thing well done in a distant part of the world; when I want a man with a good head, a good heart, lots of pluck and plenty of common sense, I always send for a captain of the Navy," Lord Palmerston claimed. His feelings reflect a typical Victorian attitude that what is needed in most critical situations is not the specialist but the amateur, not the craftsman but the man of good character; and that one's qualities as a human being count for more than special training. Applied to the navy, this myth lasted long beyond its demonstrable truth, as I shall show presently.[2]

Not only was the seaman a man of good head and good heart, he was also the representation of those qualities that made England different from other lands. One popular source claimed that Britain's greatest victories had been "won by free men, fighting gladly for England's glory, and it is by free men that the victories of the future will also be won." The fact that a man was "free," therefore, conferred on him a double advantage: it made him more skillful at his business, and it made his cause virtuous and thus inevitably victorious. Here is another illustration of the usefulness of myth: how often we see that the conviction of superior virtue endows a fighter with such supreme self-confidence that he does indeed fight better and thus win. However hard to demonstrate, it is a psychologically plausible proposition at any rate. And it may not matter whether the English seaman *was* free; the fact that he thought himself so is our concern here. The late Michael Lewis, one of England's foremost naval historians, expressed the common belief that this conviction of one's own freedom carried great weight in the outcome of England's battles. The Tudor sailor, he said, was a humble soul, but at least he *had* a soul—he was a free man. The continental sailor, particularly the Spanish galley slave, was not.[3]

But the myth not only gave the English sailor a soul, it endowed him with superior seamanship. W. Clarke Hall and Clement Salaman, in an account of a naval battle in the English Channel in 1215, described the English method of fighting as more seamanlike than the enemy's. They attributed the English success to the fact that the English ships were sailed by free men, while the foreigners used slaves; and that the English used oars only when they had contrary winds. This circumstance meant that the English standard of navigation was higher, but it also meant (more significantly to our purposes) that it fostered a spirit of independence and self-dependence unknown in foreign navies. We see the seaman functioning in two respects here, partly as the historical hero of Britain's greatness and partly as a present-day representation of national qualities most admired in the culture. One writer, for example, gave almost exclusive credit to the sailor for Britain's achievements in her upward struggle for existence, expansion, and power. In times of the greatest stress, when the whole world was at Britain's throat, the sailor stood to his quarters and fought with courage, loyalty, and devotion never surpassed.[4]

According to the myth, this spirit has been largely responsible for Britain's remarkable achievements in the world and for her position with respect to other nations. A publicist for the Navy League called the British seamen collectively "a race that has been so instrumental in building up this magnificent empire." Any other nation which was at all honest about the state of affairs would readily concede first place to the British seaman not only as navigator and fighter but, in Commander Low's words, as "the representative of a superior race." This attitude did not strike the Victorian as arrogant but simply as accurate.[5]

What were the qualities so much admired in the English seamen? They can be summed up under three headings: courage, discipline; and character. Although outstanding courage was characteristic of heroism, everyday boldness seems to have been the mark of the average seaman, and the Englishman was never surprised to find the sailor displaying a kind of pluckiness that set him apart from his fellow man. Even in circumstances where the outcome was unfortunate there was usually some quixotic quality about the men involved which would overshadow defeat. The popular children's author, Herbert Hayens, in writing about the naval loss at Santa Cruz, felt that the outcome was to some extent redeemed by the dauntless intrepidity and "optimistic bulldog courage" of the British seamen involved.[6]

Courage was so much a part of the natural equipment of the navy that its occasional absence was an event worthy of remark and deprecation. Lieut.-Colonel Knollys and Major Elliott, army officers who also wrote for children, remarked that Admiral Benbow's extraordinary courage was noteworthy not only as an example to be followed by all around him but also because the loss of his life was occasioned by the lack of courage in his captains, who had abandoned him in the fight with the French in 1702. The authors commented that the action was shadowed by what was "so seldom found as an ingredient in the character of an Englishman—cowardice."[7]

To estimate the necessary quantity of courage, a dangerous situation, preferably with mathematical odds in your enemy's favor, proves a useful dramatic backdrop. A short story, significantly titled "Heavy Odds—Ten to One: Or an Englishman's Duty," tells of a battle between an English cutter, *The Rose*, and three French brigs in the year 1795. *The Rose* was on her way to join the fleet with some important dispatches when she met the French ships and decided to fight instead of avoid them, an attack which might well be called foolhardy. There were 14 men on *The Rose* against 146 Frenchmen, and needless to say the Englishmen soundly defeated the enemy. The story ends with an acid remark about the failure of the admiralty to recognize the commanding lieutenant's heroism. Not one of the "brave fellows" received the slightest reward for the gallant manner in which they had maintained the "honor of the nation."[8]

The English fondly recounted historical as well as fictional examples of high courage in the face of danger. The famous commander of Commonwealth times, Admiral Blake, was notorious for fighting in situations where the odds were against him. In one battle with the Dutch, Blake and his partner ship (called a "plucky pair") held on like grim death, receiving and returning numerous broadsides until the Dutch retired. But one man's courage is another's idiocy or bullheaded arrogance; and one's opinion of this will certainly depend partly on which side one happens to be. Hayens also greatly admired the Tudor seaman Richard Grenville for his quick thought and outrageous boldness. He quoted with approval Grenville's opinion that an English ship should make way for no one, and stated, "It will not hurt us to remember that men of Grenville's stamp helped to make England mistress of the seas."[9]

The second quality assumed to be common to the English seaman was discipline. Discipline was closely related to courage, of course, but being the subordination of individual to group it might have been more difficult to attain. Discipline could be instilled through fear—one can beat a child into obedience—but it might also have arisen from an interior conviction of the ultimate worth of the group and of the rational superiority of its leaders. When discipline arose from this solidarity it was probably more dependable than when exacted through fear of punishment. (Of course, for survival's sake, the *comitatus* code is rigidly absolute—a tradition which goes back to and perhaps beyond the Anglo-Saxon warrior code.)

Many nineteenth-century writers commented on the extraordinary discipline of the English sailor, and the examples they instanced would seem to bear out their judgment. It is true that in the old days (until well into the mid-nineteenth century) the British tar lived a brutal existence. Beatings were common; keelhauling, cobbing, and other punishments were lavishly applied; yet in the days of Nelson it seems also to be true that the sailors obeyed a "higher" discipline—that born of confidence in their officers. There survive many examples of letters from common sailors of Nelson's time describing apparently with perfect sincerity the almost reverent awe in which the officers were held by the seamen. Perhaps it would not be surprising to find the solidarity of group displayed in time of emergency, but it was remarkable in ordinary days, too. One writer commented that the British seamen did not want to be heroes, they simply wanted to do their jobs. He attributed this workaday attitude to an important spirit that prevailed throughout the service.[10] That the British public assumed the existence of this spirit no doubt reinforced the myth for the men in the navy. One generally does tend to live up to others' expectations of his behavior, and the seaman would be as subject to the myth as the civilian.

A good example of the kind of discipline that apparently did exist is the disastrous sinking of H.M.S. *Victory*. She was rammed by H.M.S. *Camperdown* during naval maneuvers in the Mediterranean on 22 June 1893 as the result of an incorrect order given by the commanding admiral, Sir George Tryon. The men on the sinking vessel behaved perfectly; no one jumped overboard until the order was given. There was no panic; all performed their duty perfectly.[11]

In analyzing the discipline aboard the *Victory*, the journalist G. W. Steevens remarked that it was unfortunate that the junior officer, Captain Burke, did not give orders to close the watertight doors. Apparently he refrained from doing so because he was standing in the presence of his senior, Admiral Tryon. But Steevens stated, with some justice, that one may regret such perfect discipline when it means the sacrifice of personal initiative, but it is illogical to expect to have it when one wants it and dispense with it when one does not. Steevens thus raised a very important problem faced by any military or quasi-military group which depends on quick obedience, When may the individual obey without question; when must he assert his own judgment? The military journalist Spenser Wilkinson once defined discipline as the simple act of putting the best man in the lead: "Healthy men love to be led by a man whom they feel to be their superior." Provided that the navy had some reliable mechanism for identifying and appointing these "best men," such a system should succeed. But Wilkinson went on to say that it was very important to have as leaders men of good sense, and that sometimes an officer might be commended for an action which involved, strictly speaking, the countermanding of orders in the exercise of individual initiative. It is a nice judgment and an important one, and frequently it is not possible to tell the correct decision in advance.[12]

In another book Wilkinson commented that of all people it was the naval officer who was most often in such a predicament. He gave as a hypothetical example the commander of one of the queen's ships off some distant coast. There is a local disturbance, and the officer is urged to intervene and use the force at his disposal for the protection of some supposed British interest. He cannot seek instructions (in these days before radio), and he must make a quick decision. His decision—whether it be action or inaction—will later be judged by his superiors at the admiralty. If it is approved, his career will be advanced; if it is disapproved, his career will certainly suffer. The officer is bound to act on his own judgment and to take the consequences. As Wilkinson wrote, "It seems, in an age of weakness, a hard choice. But the discipline that enforces it makes men indeed, and expresses with rigorous logic the great law of all human life, that a man and his acts are one."[13]

Certainly part of the quality of discipline is the sense of responsibility which enables officer and seaman alike to devote themselves to what they call their duty. *Duty* (a popular Victorian word) involved doing one's job and making the best of circumstances. It required tasks that were unpleasant but necessary. (Sometimes *necessary* seems to have been defined by the degree of unpleasantness!) English mythology is filled with tales of people—officers great and small, the famous and the ordinary—who would have preferred, perhaps, to be home with family and hearth but instead were out on the high seas or in some distant land nobly doing their duty for queen and country. Hayens's comment on Admiral Blake is significant: in discussing Blake's illness in old age, Hayens wrote that the admiral wished he could be at home in England to die in his own bed, "but duty pointed in the opposite direction, and, true to the principle that had guided him through life, he followed it." And, "Few men have ever done so much for England; none perhaps have served her with such unselfish devotion day and night. Year in and year out, in storm and stress, he had labored incessantly, and ever his one thought had been for the honour of his country."[14]

British boys were given innumerable examples to follow; Blake was simply one of them. An article in the *Navy League Quarterly* of April 1913, significantly entitled "The Defence of the British Empire: The Duty of Every British Boy," held up for admiration the sterling figure of the king, George V. Like so many royal princes, he had had naval training. According to the author, "everyone knows our present King has been in the Navy and we have all heard how hard working he was, and he never shirked his job however dirty or disagreeable it might be."[15] The clear implication was that if a royal prince could obey this call of duty, then surely the average British boy could emulate him. Interestingly, the Victorians seemed to take unpleasantness as a kind of index of the validity of a task—the more disagreeable a job, the more worthwhile. There would be, of course, a certain interior satisfaction in not shirking; you would know from how much you disliked what you were doing that it was eminently valuable.

We find this theme of staunch devotion throughout children's literature, particularly the stirring adventure stories written for boys. The first issue of a boys' magazine called *Comrades* features a story called "A True British Sailor-Boy." The cover picture from the magazine shows a twelve-year old boy clinging to the mast of a sinking ship, with the waves lapping at his feet. The caption reads, " 'I did not desert you!' was all he said." As we know from memoirs, such literature was quite effective in persuading boys to join the navy or run away to sea with the merchant marine.[16]

The third quality of the nautical personality was character. As we shall see with respect to Nelson, it is never perfectly clear what the Victorian meant by *character*, but to some extent it summed up and included the qualities I have been discussing: courage, discipline, and devotion to duty. Character also involved truthfulness, uprightness, manliness, modesty, and what was frequently called a "great heart." Some people thought that what made a sailor such an outstanding human being was his lifelong contact with the elements. One writer, commenting on "The British Seamen: Then and Now," described the average sailor as a true comrade

63

and generous friend who had "the character which comes from kinship with the sea," a feeling which echoes that sense of mystery associated with the sea that I discussed earlier.[17]

Honor was also important; naval men were honorable men. We see the pervasiveness of this moral strain in Conrad's novel *Lord Jim*, where Jim's almost morbid sense of honor leads him to spend the major portion of his life atoning for the cardinal sin of having abandoned the passengers on his ship. Put in those terms Jim's error does seem major, given the code of the sea where the captain was in charge of the safety of ship and passengers until the very last moment of life. But Jim was a very junior officer, terrified by the imminent sinking of the old tub, which was taking water at an alarming rate. It was dark; there were not enough lifeboats for the passengers nor time to launch them; the senior officers had already abandoned the vessel. Jim lost his head and jumped overboard to join them. Some might feel his remorse was exaggerated, his atonement too much; but it bespeaks the great force of the moral ethic that a novel built on such a theme succeeds so well. Kipling's *Captains Courageous* (which might be considered a popular rather than "literary" work) also uses the sea as testing ground. This is a theme that goes back to *Beowulf* in English literature, where the sea is an arena for initiation into manhood. In *Captains Courageous*, Harvey, a weak and unattractive youth, matures to courage, honor, and manliness through his battle with the exigencies of a seafaring life. The story is American in setting but clearly harks back to Anglo-Saxon literature in time and mythic import.

Character also meant that its possessor fought for larger motives than personal glory, and indeed personal ambition was considered to be a relentless opponent of "true" character. The man of true character was a peace-loving man, but he was not a coward. British sailors were lovers of peace, but when they had to fight, they fought not for personal gain, but for the preservation of throne and country. There was some difficulty, here, in reconciling this view of the peace-loving, greathearted English sailor with the history of the Elizabethan buccaneer, who was anything but peace-loving and was frankly out for his own gain. As I shall demonstrate in my discussion of the Armada, however, one could either assume a larger patriotism on the part of the English pirates or else see a historical development of the character of the English sailor, whose origins might be traced to the Drakes and Hawkinses of the sixteenth century.

The lover of peace was magnanimous to his enemies. The British sailor never held a grudge; he was generous to his defeated opponents. He would rescue enemy sailors from drowning, after he had sunk their ship. Apparently this trait is fairly modern, but to the Victorian ethic it was important. The eighteenth-century sailors were not noted for their generosity to the enemy; a popular song about a battle with Barbary pirates contains these ironic lines:

> Oh, it was a sorry sight,
> and grieved us full sore
> to see them all a-drowning
> as they tried to swim to shore.[18]

Since, in early warfare, quarter was neither given nor asked, it is perhaps not surprising that the sailor was ruthless. It was all the more remarkable, then, when the sailors of Nelson's fleet were often described as ministering to wounded French sailors.

One element in the myth of the sailor was the conviction that on the whole the sailor was unappreciated. The man of character and honor was also a modest man, not given to boasting of his exploits. He was therefore frequently overlooked by his superiors and, as I remarked earlier, had to take his satisfactions from the sense of a job well done. According to popular belief, officialdom was always blind, stupid, and unappreciative of both the sailor's achievements and his difficulties. The people in Whitehall, who never had the advantage of the excitement and exhilaration of the battlefield, were prevented thereby from a true understanding of the value and self-sacrifice of the mariner and thus could never give credit where it was due. They were often small-minded, too, unwilling to reward obvious virtue.

Knollys's and Elliott's description of Dundonald's treatment at the hands of his superiors stressed the malice of those at the admiralty and exclaimed, "Whose blood would not be fired—what honest man, loving truth and justice, would not be indignant—at the recollection of the infamy cast upon the history of this country by the conduct of those ministers—all honorable men, forsooth, who so relentlessly persecuted one of the greatest naval heroes, one of the most pure-minded, honorable men whom this nation has ever produced?"[19] And if Dundonald, one of the great English heroes, received such treatment, what could one expect for the more ordinary men, those of lesser fame? This view of officialdom was a very common one and frequently featured in the fiction of the period. Gilbert's and Sullivan's treatment of the admiralty in their comic operetta *H.M.S. Pinafore* was not unusual. Sir Joseph Porter's qualifications for being "ruler of the Queen's navy" were, as he candidly tells us, good handwriting, an attention to brass polishing, and a refusal ever to set foot on board ship.

Although the Englishman would probably have conceded that the seagoing life of late-Victorian times was tame in comparison to the good old days, he nevertheless assumed that there was something particularly exciting about a naval career that poor landsmen could only envy. The popular ballads of the eighteenth century were still sung in the nineteenth century and probably still reflected the Victorian picture of the sailor. The jolly tar of the myth was carefree, inured to hardship, contemptuous of danger, strong, and healthy; although some people objected that eighteenth-century ballads did not do justice to the sailor. The greatest sinner apparently was Charles Dibdin. One writer complained that Dibdin's verse painted Sailor Jack as a vulgar buffoon: "Can anyone believe that the Empire was won by the sort of drunken, stupid mountebank who pervades the sea songs of that period, bawling for grog or 'swizzy,' talking rubbish about Poll, Sue, and Nancy, and even greater rubbish about marling spikes and maintopbraces?" Clark Russell also found Dibdin's verse unfortunate, particularly as it represented the sort of poet who sprinkled his verse liberally with "Pull away boys," and "heave ho" to give a nautical flavor to landlubberish verse. Russell was scornful of Dibdin's total lack of real knowledge. But if people read Dibdin, as they apparently did, and were affected by him, then we must acknowledge him as myth-maker, however ignorant of the sea he may have been.[20]

A modern writer, naval expert, and historian has commented that it was as a result of the naval victories and their celebration in eighteenth-century verse that much of the nineteenth-century tradition was established: "Life at sea might be hard and unpopular, but at least the seaman was led by officers of outstanding ability, and he had the satisfaction of knowing that in his country's estimation he was a national hero, a 'heart of oak,' who maintained the tradition expressed in Garrick's chorus: 'We'll fight and we'll conquer again and again.' " As Garrick wrote, "For who are so free as the sons of the waves?/Heart of Oak are our ships; heart of oak are our men." A footnote to the quotation of this poem in an anthology alleges that the term *Hearts of Oak* (plural) was old in Garrick's day. The editor traces it back to the early seventeenth century, and he gives instances of the phrase in the intervening years before Garrick wrote the song to which William Boyce wrote the music in the late eighteenth century.[21]

The actual (as opposed to mythic) conditions under which these pre-Victorian sailors lived gradually became known in the nineteenth century and were shocking, even in a time which was less easily disturbed by squalor and disease than we like to think ourselves today. Frederick Marryat's novels, for example, were influential in acquainting the public with the ill-fed, ill-paid, ill-housed life of the common sailor, who was subject to a discipline incredibly severe by any standards.

Gradual reform came about in part because of a shortage of naval personnel created by increasing opportunities in less dangerous and more attractive fields open to the poor lad of humble origins. The image persisted, however (and probably affected recruits as well as landlubbers), that the sailor's life, for all its hardship, was glamorous and fun. He had a girl in every port, no tiresome domestic responsibilities, and the encouraging sense that his job was vital to the freedom and safety of his whole nation. Small wonder, then, that the landsman often envied the sailor and sang songs like this:

> A Sailor's life's a life of woe,
>   He works now late, now early,
> Now up and down, now to and fro,
>   What then? he takes it cheerly:
> Bless'd with a smiling can of grog,
>   If duty call,
>   Stand, rise, or fall,
> To fate's last verge he'll jog:
>   The cadge to weigh,
>   The sheets belay,
> He does it with a wish!
>   To heave the lead,
>   Or to cat-head
> The pondrous anchor fish:
>   For while the grog goes round,
>   All sense of danger drown'd
>   We despise it to a man:
> We sing a little, we laugh a little,
> And work a little, and swear a little,
>   And swing the flowing can.[22]

Much of the landsman's view of the sailing life was based on truth —the sailor often did live a carefree, irresponsible, reckless life;

67

he often was the brawling, sex-starved, rowdy creature of song and story. The point here is not the historical truth or falsehood of such an image, but the fact that the image itself existed and that it was believed.

In all this discussion of the sterling qualities of the nautical Englishman nowhere have I mentioned what might be considered paramount: his seamanship. Curiously enough, until quite late in the nineteenth century mere skill with ships seemed the least important concern. The myth extolled courage, daring, enterprise, and character; but we find little mention of sailing ability. The exception to this rule came when English seamen were compared with foreigners, and then, frequently, their superiority as sailors was attributed not to exact training but to their inborn virtues as human beings. Time and again the literature dwelt on historical as well as fictional incidents when the extra resourcefulness and extra devotion of the British seaman meant an advantage in a battle or an emergency situation. Professor Laughton described one such battle in August 1805 between a French ship, the *Didon*, and the English ship, the *Phoenix*. The two ships were heavily damaged by the fight, but the *Phoenix* repaired herself more quickly because her "splendid ship's company" could splice ropes and mend sails with more speed than their French counterparts: "It was in fact this power of recovery that so often gave us a great advantage. The very best of the French crews were never able to equal ours in this respect."[23] Clearly, Laughton's confidence lay in the skill born of spirit rather than of superior training. English sailors were better than French because they were more plucky and because they were born free men in a free country—a considerable difference.

A short story in *Pearsons*, a popular family magazine, told of a British destroyer's commander, a member of a British blockading fleet, who craved a little action. Two enemy destroyers had come out of the blockaded harbor and were sunk by the British ship. The captured men, rescued from the waters, revealed that the harbor boom was going to be withdrawn. The British officer determined to go into the harbor under cover of darkness, destroy several ships, and then escape to his own fleet. He did so, covering himself and his ship with appropriate glory. It is a brief but exciting tale, with many of the elements of the sailor myth: the pluck of the commander, his daring and resourcefulness, the heavy odds against him, and the despicable cowardice of the enemy contrasted to the "brave little destroyer" which dared to risk all for an important advantage.[24] (The enemy is not identified, but it is presumably Germany since, although Britain was not yet in the First World War, Germany had by that time [1914] emerged as the potential antagonist.)

⁕   ⁕   ⁕

Clearly in contemporary Victorian England the navy was considered a worthy career. It was a profession suitable for rich or poor that (in theory, at any rate) rewarded spirit, enterprise, and skill. When we examine naval training to see where these qualities came from, an anomaly immediately surprises us: it is unclear whether boys of great character (the "best of the race") inevitably entered the navy, or that the navy instilled good character in those fortunate enough to choose its training. Many people believe both at the same time. The *Times* stated firmly that the sea service was, from its very nature, an "almost incomparable school" for the formation of character. The navy took boys when they were very young and subjected them to the difficulty, responsibility, and danger of a very arduous profession. It endowed them with experience beyond their years, inuring them to habits of strict discipline and responsibilities of command. In addition, the boys lived under conditions of a hard and healthy life, with plenty of work but with frequent opportunities for wholesome recreation. The result was a man who turned with instant readiness from pleasure to duty, from dalliance to danger, and the resulting character could hardly be improved upon. (The editorial, in fact, reads like a particularly fulsome brochure for a boarding school!)[25]

The emphasis on those qualities of character training—hard work, discipline, a healthy outdoor life with plenty of "games"—is characteristic of the pervasiveness of the British myth of the public school ethos as well. In addition to hard work and team sports, however, we find the assumption that somehow it was healthier to live on sea than on land, that the constant contact with the vicissitudes of naval life added an extra measure to the training. A Navy League pamphlet suggested that the best training for boys was contact with "the mighty forces of nature." Other good influences were temporary absence from home and ready submission to the will of others for the general good.[29] (Deprivation being good for the soul was so striking an idea that I wonder to what extent national life and policy were framed by such an attitude.)

This same pamphlet goes on to laud the dignity which comes from serving in a grand cause, as well as patience, love of order,

69

and self-control. It was important, however, to catch a boy when he was young. Most of the boys who were trained for naval service started as early as age thirteen or fourteen. The theory was to get a boy before he had the opportunity to be influenced by ordinary life. The earlier a boy was trained to love the sea, the more certain and permanent would be those feelings. But it was also possible to use the navy as a corrective for bad early influences. One amusing short story told of a boy named Tom Giles, who was a member of a London city gang called the Roarers, whose chief delight was to throw stones and mud at passersby. One day the Roarers assaulted a gentleman who happened to be an admiral in mufti. The gentleman counterattacked; and although the gang fled he managed to capture one of the boys, the unfortunate Tom. The upshot of the story was that Tom was persuaded· to abandon his evil ways and go into naval training, "a-serving of King and Country." Tom's life then turned from bad to good and he was henceforth a credit to his nation.[27]

There was some objection to the use of the navy as a kind of national reform school; some people disliked the idea that it was a place for "bad boys" and deplored such a stigma attached to naval training. One naval captain argued that city slums were not a good source of manpower, chiefly because such boys had been brought up on poor food and, even worse, on poor moral standards. He thought that the three most important requisites were a good physique, intelligence, and an aptitude for sea life. He failed, however, to supply details on how such aptitude could be determined in advance. A Navy League member also argued that it was more important to have good rather than poor quality men join the navy; so much depended on the navy as a national symbol. She placed great confidence in heredity, arguing that the middle classes were the best source of manpower, since it was the middle classes who had formed the national "backbone" in England's history and created characters full of intelligence, self-respect, and manly self-dependence. "We want lads for the Royal Navy to be taken from the best stocks." The admirality encouraged parents to send a son into the navy if the boy were "resourceful, resolute, quick to decide, and ready to act on his own decision, . . . no slacker, but keen in work and play . . . sound in wind and limb . . . cheerful, unselfish, and considerate . . . responsive and observant . . . master of himself . . . and able to learn the secret of command through the discipline of obedience."[28]

70

Although there was confusion over whether the navy represented character or instilled character, there was no great disagreement on the kind of training these boys should receive. Spenser
Wilkinson thought that a public school education was unnecessary
for naval officers, because public schools provided only two things:
a knowledge of the classics (which would be useless) and the experience of group living with tradition and discipline—an experience better acquired in the service itself. Wilkinson proposed that
at the age of thirteen a boy be sent to the training yacht *Britannia*
for four years; thence to sea as a midshipman for five or six years
to learn each department of naval skill in turn; thence to naval
college for a year, from which he would graduate as an officer.
According to Wilkinson, a naval officer should be familiar with the
sea and all its ways; he should be familiar with his own ship; but
most of all he should be a leader of men, able to command, and
a master of tactics and strategy.[29]

Adults conceived of life aboard a training ship in glowing terms
and as happy and healthy: happy because it was healthy, and
healthy because the boys were well fed, active, hard-working, and
cooperative.[30] Some of this rosy glow could surely have been attributed to that common adult nostalgia about carefree youth. But
there was more, too, that connected this training with the romantic
vision of the influences of the sea. The idealizing of naval life seems
to have made little distinction between the officer and the common
tar. Many of the qualities that I have been discussing refer to both
sorts of men; and although specific schooling would have been re-
served for the officer class, it was assumed that the seamen bene-
fited from the examples set them.

Training in the years before 1860 had been considerably hit-
or-miss. In 1868, in response to complaints, a more rationally
organized system was established, centering on the use of training
ships. There was a serious shortage of personnel, and the modern
competition with other navies suggested that improvements were
vital if Britain were to keep its place. Accordingly, the government
authorized improvement of the living conditions, the pay, and the
terms of service. In 1903 a program called the *New Scheme* was
inaugurated. The curriculum was modernized to include more math-
ematics and science, engineering, seamanship, and sailing; but
also history, foreign languages, religion, and "games." The aim was
a Public School training along naval lines. But despite changes, the
admiralty was always worried about a shortage of men. As a par-

71

allel to the periodic scares about the size of the fleet, there were minor scares about the problem of manning what new ships could be built.

The problem was this: How could you have a naval service that would not be prohibitively expensive to support in peacetime and yet would be adequate for wartime needs? In 1896 Sir Charles Beresford proposed to shorten the service time from twelve years' minimum to five and then pass men into the reserve where they would then be available on short notice in case of emergency. It thus would not be necessary to carry them on full pay in peacetime. The first lord of the admiralty, Mr. Goschen, wanted to man the fleet in wartime with pensioners; but, as the journalist G. W. Steevens pointed out, this would not be a workable scheme since the number of pensioners was small, the men overage and perhaps not so useful as younger personnel would be. In the old days, of course, the press-gang had sufficed. In the Nelson period the bounty system was in use, but it had been condemned in the mid-nineteenth century as both immoral and expensive. Under the bounty system, apparently, many men entered the service, collected their money, deserted, and then reenlisted to collect all over again. Steevens himself thought it would be possible to increase the Royal Naval Reserve, but the difficulty with depending on the reserve system was that most men in the reserve were insufficiently trained for the complicated work of modern warfare.[31]

The standard source on which the navy had relied in wartime emergencies was the mercantile marine. Alas for British self-esteem, the late-Victorian merchant marine was largely filled with foreigners! According to some estimates, only 34,000 (54 percent) of the 63,000 men in the merchant marine were British. The idea of having to depend on foreigners in time of war was unthinkable. As Commander Low put it in a long poem called "Britannia's Bulwarks," "And foreigners, and all the scum/Of seaport towns, when troubles come/Will leave us in the lurch." Of course, foreigners were employed in the merchant marine largely because they were willing to serve for lower wages than English seamen. They accepted inferior food and conditions; apparently service in the British mercantile marine was, even so, significantly better than in those of other nations. Some owners of merchant shipping would have preferred using British to foreign sailors, but these were simply not available.[32]

The trouble was that foreigners were noticeably less reliable as sailors. Dr. Macaulay, who wrote adventure stories for children, gave an account of a true case of mutiny on an American ship which had come about as a direct result of employing too many foreign seamen. The parallel to, and moral for, the British situation was obvious. He claimed that it was not uncommon for a single British merchant ship to have over half of its crew foreign, a situation that constituted "one of the grievances and perils of the present time." None of these foreigners, he said, came up to the standard of British seamen; and although they had many good qualities, "the Briton will, however, do more hard work of any kind, and do it better; he will be less dismayed in time of danger; he will struggle on longer, and die harder at the last, faithful to the end. All the best qualities of the grand race to which he belongs are still to be found in him." He felt that if British seamen were better paid and treated by their employers, the result would have been a merchant navy that would regain the high character that it had been losing for some time.[33]

Unfortunately, the merchant marine had none of the prestige of the Royal Navy. Commander Crutchley's comparison of the British fleet with the German fleet argued that in Germany the mercantile marine was considered quite an honorable profession, as it was not in Britain. The author thought that the solution to the problem of shortage of personnel was to improve conditions in the merchant marine and to stop using ships as reformatories: the sea required the best men, not the worst. Officers in the mercantile marine should have to be made equivalent to the officers in the Royal Navy. The novelist W. Clark Russell agreed. In the old days (the early nineteenth century), the merchant marine and the navy used to be interdependent: Merchant Jack helped to win Britain's greatest victories. But now all was changed; the merchant marine was filled with foreigners "who are of no earthly use to us as a fighting element." Russell called the shipowners who hired non-British seaman "traitors" (this was rather strong but fairly typical language).[34]

British attitudes toward foreigners were commonly contemptuous, but the contempt had a special flavor in this case, given the British assumption of proprietorship over the seven seas. Sometimes there was a gracious condescension toward rivals: "Probably all are our equals in bravery—it would, at least, be discourteous and unwarrantable to presume otherwise—almost certainly all are our inferiors in seamanship." The Russian was well disciplined but "intelligence is not [his] strong point." The German was well drilled but did not have enough experience at sea; the Italian was ill trained; the

73

American disobedient. Only the Frenchman was a serious threat. In any case, one could never be sure how a man would behave in the heat of battle—only the British bluejacket had proved his worth. Another author claimed that the serious crimes in the merchant service were invariably committed by the foreigners, particularly those of Latin races. Fred Jane, author of *Jane's Fighting Ships*, also believed that the Russian seamen were easily commanded because they were "not very intelligent," although "boyish" and willing to work.[35]

If the merchant marine were staffed with such unstable sorts, it would be folly to expect them to defend Britain. But of course the principal objection to using merchant seamen in time of war was that modern warfare and modern warships required much more professional training than they had in the good old days. Weapons and equipment on contemporary battleships and destroyers needed exact skill; no longer were a stout heart in a sturdy body, plenty of pluck, determination, and loyalty adequate for fighting Britain's enemies. It was some time, however, before the myth caught up with the facts of modern warfare. Earlier in the century, when Britain began to change from the wooden navy to the new ironclad vessels, there was some head-shaking about the loss of enterprise and dash in the British sailor, who now would be little more than simply a beast of burden. Naval writers reassured the public. They pointed out that one of the chief attractions of a naval career had always been the great opportunity to exercise judgment and initiative, and that these opportunities existed in even greater measure at that time than in the days of Nelson, precisely because the service and the equipment were more complicated, and naval warfare more complex.

In the introduction to his very popular book, *Eminent Sailors*, W. H. Davenport Adams condemned the curious assumption that an Englishman would fight less gallantly on an ironclad than on a wooden ship of war. Certainly the records did not show British seamen failing in their traditional spirit. Why do people apologize for the present-day navy? he asked. Perhaps the reason was the strong contrast between the seamen of Victorian and Georgian England. The Jack Tar of the eighteenth century, he continued, would be unknown today. There was very little affinity between the rollicking, boisterous, oath-taking mariner of Marryat and the contemporary sober, hard-working British seaman. People apparently assumed that because he had changed so much in outward behavior he was therefore a man of different mettle when it came to fighting. Not so, said Adams; Jack was as brave and faithful, as loyal and generous as ever; he had simply thrown off the "dregs and dross of his coarser nature." Sir William Laird Clowes, a well known popular writer on naval affairs, agreed with Adams. The modern British seaman, even when he was enjoying himself ashore, was no longer the drunken, dissipated, "utterly improvident fellow" that his great grandfather had been; and of course he was better educated. He was, moreover, neater and more decent in his habits. But he was the same, goodnatured, cheery, openhearted, childlike soul, ever ready to do his duty, never afraid of hard work, and still proud of the grand traditions of his service.[36]

Gradually the public came to accept that the introduction of mechanized warfare meant a need for greater skill rather than the reverse. In the days of the shift from sail to steam people used to complain that such a change would demoralize the crew, but they had been proved wrong. Similarly, the *Standard* commented, while the old sailing ship commanded a strong arm and a stout heart, the present-day submarine service needed precisely those qualities in even greater measure: "Nearly all sailors are brave; but those who volunteer for the submarine service may be called without exaggeration heroes."[37] The general distaste for the submarine may have lain in the feeling that it was simply a submerged box wherein lay no opportunity for individuals to be heroic. Considering the great hazards of the service (even more so then than now, when navigational and defensive aids are more fully developed), the newspaper's label was probably accurate.

But some of the worry about the present and nostalgia for the past continued. In 1901 a naval lieutenant wrote that the adoption of the torpedo would have a beneficial effect on the navy, since it would be the means of supplying the younger officers with a "fresh outlet for display of dash and enterprise." Nothing could equal the feeling of exaltation that arose in the heart of an officer who successfully delivered a torpedo into the side of an enemy ship and watched the vessel slowly sinking, the victim of his skill and daring. The torpedo had thus brought "fresh zest into the navy."[38] Bloodthirsty as this sounds, it should be understood as a poignant backward look at a time when correctly or incorrectly the navy was seen as the stage for the individual; the simpler, more robust era of the Victorian seaman, true descendent of his Elizabethan ancestors, who showed the courage and contempt for danger worthy of the best of the race.

The British Tar in Fact and Fiction is a good illustration of the

75

Victorian myths of the sailor. In a wide-ranging survey of history, literature, biography, poetry, and journalism, the author, Commander Robinson, attempted to draw an accurate portrait of the "poetry, pathos, and humour of the sailor's life" and in the process unconsciously expressed so many of the myths we have been discussing: the bravery, loyalty, hardihood and skill of the British tar and his officers. Robinson's book is dedicated to the brotherhood of the sea, and his preface declares that it was written not only for the young men who are entering naval life, "but for all who realise the importance to the British Empire of the Navy which protects its communications and guards its heart."[39]

The word *heart* is significant here because it signals the very deep kinship, the intense emotional bond between the English and the sea, the assumption that was so well expressed over thirty years earlier by Robert Louis Stevenson: "The sea is our approach and bulwark; it has been the scene of our greatest triumphs and dangers; and we are accustomed in lyrical strains to claim it as our own. . . . We should consider ourselves unworthy of our descent if we did not share the arrogance of our progenitors and please ourselves with the pretension that the sea is English."[40] Probably, as Stevenson implied, deep in the heart of every Englishman lay the image of the navy as one lone, billowy sailed ship manned by one stouthearted seaman in mortal combat against the elements and England's foes. It took a great effort of the imagination to reconcile this deeply satisfying myth with the realities of great fleets of coal-powered monsters run by machines and tended by brainless automata. The nostalgia for a day when an individual commander could sink a single enemy ship clearly reflects this attitude. Myths do not vanish suddenly; they are eroded by time. But even today the navy is called the *senior service*. It would not be surprising to find much of the general public still believing with one naval officer who wrote in 1896 that there was no nobler career that could be adopted than one "which has never failed the country in time of need and always puts before it as a guide the simple, but sufficient signal 'England expects that every man will do his duty.' "[41]

6

The Victorian Myths of the Armada

We may be sure the English courage never wavered, not for an instant. The greater the danger, the higher rose the indomitable English spirit.

J. C. Hadden, *Boy's Book of the Navy*

O noble England fall doune upon thy knee
And praise thy God with thankfull hart
Which still maintaineth thee.

from a contemporary Armada ballad

IN MY DISCUSSION IN CHAPTER 4, I NOTED THAT INVASION SEEMS A particular terror for an island nation. Britain had been invaded many times in its long history, but never since the coming of the Normans in 1066 had she been conquered by another power. Thus it is not surprising to see that for the modern Englishman the story of the defeat of Philip II's attempted invasion in 1588 had a special thrill. The mythology of the Armada contained a number of elements which contributed to the Victorian self-image and were exemplified in James Anthony Froude's treatment of six-teenth-century history. His work, published at the height of the British hegemony, illustrated most of the features of the invasion myth and will serve as a useful mirror for a discussion of that myth.

Froude, who was born in 1818, was educated at Westminster and at Oriel College, Oxford, and was elected to a fellowship at Exeter in 1842. He was up at Oxford at the height of the Trac-tarian religious revival and joined the High Church party, becoming a deacon in 1845. His religious opinions began to shift in the forties; he resigned his fellowship under some pressure and devoted his attention to his monumental work, *History of England from the Fall of Wolsey to the Defeat of the Spanish Armada,* the first two volumes of which appeared in 1850. The twelfth and final volume appeared in 1870. The central theme of Froude's history was the significance of the Reformation as "the root and source of the expansive force which has spread the Anglo-Saxon race over the globe." Froude considered "the breaking of the bonds of Rome" as the greatest achievement in English history, not least because he saw it as a bloodless revolution, in contrast to the story in every other major European country. He believed that King Philip of Spain had planned the invasion of England not only to regain the English throne lost when his wife Mary Tudor died, but also to bring England back into the Catholic fold. For Froude, as for a number of Victorians, the Catholic church was still the "scarlet woman" and the "whore of Rome," a reactionary, illiberal power which represented the forces of Darkness. Protestantism, particularly Anglicanism, was by contrast the agent of Good, of progress, of freedom and national self-fulfillment. It was not accidental, therefore, that Froude did not continue his history through 1603, the end of the Tudors, but chose instead to draw the curtains at the conclusion of the Armada battle in 1588. His work by its terminal dates is more a history of the English Reformation than of the nation as a whole; he saw 1588 as representing the final success of Anglicanism, a conclusion that many subsequent historians might dispute.

Froude's great gift as a historian was his power of narrative; no one could read his treatment of the execution of Mary, Queen of Scots without being móved by its poignancy. His characters lived with a timeless vitality, and his feeling for the dramatic sweep of the historical past made him popular with the English reading public. His attitude toward history was more that of a stage manager or impresario than a meticulous and objective observer of the past. Consequently he used to take liberties with his sources that most historians today would find appalling. It is not in the role of reliable historian that we use him here, however, but as Victorian myth maker.

Two great sets of Victorian myths emerged from the story of the Armada. The first concerned the naval lessons of the victory over the Spanish, and the second developed the Armada as the original source of the greatness of English seamanship, as exemplified by the models of Drake and Hawkins. Froude dealt with these two myths *in extenso,* both in his twelve-volume history and in his other works, in particular a series of lectures given at Oxford after his appointment as Regius Professor of Modern History in 1892. These nine lectures were published as *English Seamen in the Sixteenth Century*, the first of which had the significant title "The Sea Cradle of the Reformation." It was Froude's contention that the development of an English "navy" was largely attributable to Henry VIII's defensive needs after his break with Rome.

Thus the navy came into being, according to Froude, as both an agent of, and a result of, the Reformation. He pointed out that when Elizabeth came to the English throne in 1558, Sir William Cecil, her minister, saw at once that it was on the navy that the prosperity and "even the liberty of England must eventually depend."[1] If England were to remain Protestant she could be saved from the Catholic powers not by Acts of Uniformity but only by a strong fleet. Froude's work typifies the nineteenth-century habit of projecting contemporary conclusions onto the past and illustrates a need to reinforce myth with the weight of history. Again, we should emphasize that it may very well have been true that Cecil saw the fleet as the savior of English liberty and prosperity, but such fact has only a tangential bearing on the Victorian mythology. Cecil's beliefs could be part of the Elizabethan myths, but the historians' *use* of his ideas would serve to reinforce the Victorian myth.

The story of the Armada was familiar to the smallest English schoolchild. Although the details may have varied from version to version, many elements remained basic, and all accounts had the following elements: King Philip of Spain evilly plots his invasion; the Duke of Medina-Sidonia gathers a great fleet and finally sets sail; Drake and Howard play bowls on the Hoe at Plymouth, awaiting the coming of the Spanish; the English encounter the Armada in the Channel; there is a desperate shortage of supplies; the little English ships fight a terrible battle against the mammoth Spanish galleons; Drake uses fireships; and finally there is a fierce storm that disperses the enemy and ends the king's dreams of conquest. By most accounts, when Howard (the lord high admiral) and Drake set sail from Plymouth to intercept the Spanish fleet, they had not yet their full complement of ships and men and thus were determined to avoid a risky pitched battle with the Armada. They decided instead to hang onto the edges of the flotilla, harrassing the Spanish until the arrival of Lord Henry Seymour's reinforcements. The giant Armada sailed majestically up the channel in a crescent formation seven miles long. Although at first Drake and Howard could not afford to engage the enemy directly, they managed to stay on his flanks out of gun range as the Duke of

Medina-Sidonia made for the port of Calais, where he had been ordered to pick up the Duke of Parma's army. As one writer characteristically described the scene, the English captains sailed "round and round the unwieldy mass of Spanish shipping, like bees around a furious bull, pausing often to inflict their sting and then darting off before they could be punished for their boldness."[2] The image of David attacking Goliath was popular, and the metaphor particularly pleased the English imagination, which was fond of the underdog's role and delighted in fighting against "heavy odds."

Victorian historians disagreed widely on the relative strength of the two fleets, but all emphasized that the Spanish had the advantage in numbers and total tonnage. The discrepancies in detail might be attributable to a simple difficulty in counting. On one or two days of the battle the English fleet was amplified by amateur craft manned by fishermen who put out from the various seaports on the Channel to help in any way they could. As Froude described these loyal subjects, he wrote that it was the business of their lives "to meet the enemies of their land and their faith on the wide ocean."[3] Whether this volunteer navy was a help or a hindrance to the commander is perhaps questionable, but the myth that glorifies the role of the amateur can profit either way. In any case, whatever the precise total of ships, it was generally accepted that the Spanish outnumbered the English by about four to one. The English, however, were not at such a disadvantage as numbers would suggest. The Spanish galleons and galleasses were very large, full of troops, and cumbersome compared to the English ships.

The queen's place in the story is similarly important to the historical imagination, which makes a great deal of the phrase "Elizabethan England" as a symbol of the unification of the land. Again, it is hard to tell in reality how much sense of national unity actually existed in sixteenth-century England, but the nineteenth-century historians dwelt upon it, and it became part of the myth. Most accounts made much of the picture of the queen riding out to see her soldiers and ships, and of her giving customarily well phrased, encouraging speeches to her people. As one popular children's history described it, the people of England showed their queen how they might be trusted, coming willingly to volunteer as sailors and soldiers, donating money for supplies, and supporting the queen in every way possible. Froude remarked, however, it was well for England that she had other defenders than "the wildly managed navy of the queen."[4]

Elizabeth's stinginess was notorious, and there was scarcely a writer who could forbear to point out that her parsimony with supplies very nearly cost the English the battle. Froude himself dwelt on how much the queen would have preferred a diplomatic settlement simply to save money; at no time did the fleet have more than three or four weeks' supplies in hand and was frequently down to half-rations. The queen refused to allow more than two days' gunpowder and frequently chided her men for wasting shot in gunnery practice. Yet somehow, in spite of these difficulties, the morale of the English sailors remained very high: "They were ill-clothed, ill-provided in every way, but they complained of nothing, caught fish to mend their mess dinners, prayed for the speedy coming of the enemy. [But] even Howard's heart failed him now. English sailors would do what could be done by man, but they could not fight with famine."[5] Lord Howard implored the queen to order more supplies, and eventually she gave in. The queen's penury may have made her lovably human, but it also served to magnify the eventual victory since the difficulties she created were overcome by the superior spirit of the people.

The Victorians ascribed the defeat of the Armada to a number of reasons, each interesting in its implications. One popular explanation attributed the victory to the terrible storm that dispersed the Spanish fleet. This so-called Protestant wind was seen as a judgment of God upon the Spanish for their wicked designs on England. It was certainly responsible for the perils that came upon the Spanish ships as they struggled northward around Scotland and hopefully homeward. But there had also been a great battle in the Channel before the storm, and due credit had to be allowed to the skill, courage, and daring of the English and their commanders. W. H. Davenport Adams, who wrote a very popular history of the British Navy, put it succinctly: "If the storm and the tempest ruined the Armada, Drake and his comrades had already *defeated* it."[6]

In another explanation, an Edwardian boys' book, *The Sea and Its Story*, attributed the defeat of the Armada to the unmaneuverability of the huge Spanish vessels, although conceding that the storm finished the job by demoralizing and immobilizing the enemy. In his biography of Howard, the naval historian John Knox Laughton contended that the advantage had always lain with the English because they had learned to trust off-fighting and quick movement. Spain had better-equipped armies and liked to fight on the sea by grappling and fighting at close hand. Another author also

81

stressed the contrast between English and Spanish ships, remarking that the fixed guns could not get a bearing on the "well-handled, smaller, but better-armed English ships."[7]

Generally, Victorian historians made very little of the difficulties faced by the Spanish from the early weather, from insufficient supplies, and from inadequate preparation. (Such causes, of course, would not particularly redound to the English credit.) Adams thought that the Spanish probably felt that at last they had met the men who would wrest from them the supremacy of the seas, men who were "as much their superiors in tenacity and patience and the higher courage as in nautical skill." Adams emphasized that it was really "spirit" that had won the battle. He described the English volunteers turning up in all sorts of little craft, a sight which today might remind us of Dunkirk in 1940. He thought that these volunteers did not add any real strength, but that their enthusiastic spirit contributed a spiritual strength to the half-starved, neglected crews of the fleet and gave them a sense that the "heart of England" was with them, thus transforming every common seaman into a hero.[8]

Whether it was Spanish weakness or English togetherness, the fact remained that the Armada had been shattered, the threat of invasion postponed. The Spanish ships could not return to Spain through the Straits of Dover. The wind was against them, and hostile vessels lurked in every port. They had, therefore, to beat a terrible passage through the North Sea and around the Scottish coast, where they encountered a good deal of bad weather and considerable unfriendliness from the Irish.

Such is the picture of the Armada story drawn by Victorian mythologizing. The lessons reinforce the Victorian naval myth: trust to courage, devoted amateurs, and plucky little ships. The other half of the Armada myth is the effect that the battle had on the development of the English seaman. These were the days before the establishment of a professional navy, and the queen's service was manned by innumerable private sailors, people engaged either in fishing or in trade for their own profit. The bulk of the personnel for the navy had to be recruited from these privateers. According to Froude, privateering suited the queen's convenience and her disposition. It certainly was less expensive than the maintenance of professional seamen. The queen liked men who would do her work without being paid for it, men whom she could "disown when expedient; who would understand her, and would not resent it." The writer of a boys' naval history of England agreed.

In discussing Hawkins, Drake, Frobisher, and Cumberland, he remarked that it was mainly in "this splendid school for seamanship" that the queen's most brilliant naval leaders learned their lessons, stressing the "pluck" and "hardihood" of those old sea dogs, common terms of approval in the popular culture. It was very lucky for England that in her hour of need she had bred such a "strong and virile race." One finds this emphasis on the racial qualities of English seamen in many places. Speaking of the Elizabethan seamen, a schoolmaster at Tonbridge wrote of their courage and adventurous spirit, which he claimed "helped to found a race of seamen that no other nation could equal." Men like Drake were quite ready for adventure and were not always overscrupulous as to where their adventure took them.[9]

Tennyson's poem "The Revenge" illustrates these qualities in profusion. Sir Richard Grenville lost a skirmish with the Spanish in 1591 and behaved with such reckless courage that even the enemy were impressed. Mortally wounded, and captured at last, Sir Richard was laid on the deck by the mast,

> And they praised him to his face with their
>   courtly foreign grace;
> But he rose upon their decks, and he cried:
> "I have fought for Queen and Faith like a
>   valiant man and true;
> I have only done my duty as a man is bound
>   to do.
> With a joyful spirit I Sir Richard Grenville die!"
> And he fell upon their decks, and he died.

The Victorian moral code struggled with this problem of piracy, admiring the boldness and trying to admire the results but disapproving of the undoubted illegality of the buccaneers' adventures. One author stated rather lamely that whether or not the Drakes and Hawkinses were genuine traders or bold buccaneers, "there is no doubt that they were skilled mariners and had no rivals in seamanship." This was certainly meant as a compliment and tended to take the sting out of the connotation of piracy, but the moral problem remained. A naval commander's book, *Privateers and Privateering*, defined privateers as "licensed plunderers" and pirates as "unlicensed." He admits that since plunder, not patriotism, had been the general rule of these privateers, it was often hard to distinguish the two, but he conveys the feeling that privateering was the more romantic business. Froude is more forthright: privateers were plainly the armed force of the nation; their peacetime name of *pirate* was unimportant. Certainly the general tone of the Victorian writers approved the overriding concerns of national safety instead of condemning theft on the high seas. A popular boys' book described sailors as "springing up on every hand" in response to the need. Although these men were pirates in practice, their names were justly honored because they stood for something large—the making of the British Navy. It was the heroic type that was admired here: daring, courage, and resourcefulness— the moral code was perhaps rightly laid aside as irrelevant.[10]

There were four other methods by which Victorian writers got around this difficult problem of illegal behavior. One pointed out that sea piracy was an important school that taught the needed qualities of courage, skill, and endurance in the English seaman. These pirates also had lofty motives: Drake and Hawkins were inspired by religion and patriotism much more strongly than by their love of gold. A second method called Drake, Hawkins, and their kin "pirates" in deed but "of a very fine and heroic order, into whose motives was infused a certain nobility of purpose." A third way to approve a less-than-admirable quality was to claim that everybody was doing it. One writer conceded that a generous and honorable man should perhaps have preferred some other path to wealth than the slave trade, but while Hawkins was not *more* generous or honorable than his colleagues, he certainly was no worse. And it was true that piracy was a venerable institution not yet condemned by Christian morality. In wartime it was openly sanctioned; in peacetime it was only slightly denounced, and then only when it seemed likely to result in unwelcome war.[11]

Finally, historians argued that England's enemies had it coming to them. English seamen had suffered cruel outrages at the hands of French and Spanish privateers. The spirit of adventure and the booty to be obtained in reprisal would have tempted men of even the highest moral stature. Two writers justified English piratical behavior on the grounds that Spain was too wealthy and that she had been playing the international bully with the poor little Netherlands. She therefore deserved whatever she got. In reference to Cavendish's piracy, one author remarked that, like Drake, Cavendish considered himself a chosen messenger to visit God's wrath upon the Spanish devils.[12] This image of the nation as agent of divine justice was not, of course, confined to nineteenth-century England; throughout history various peoples have assumed that they were God's chosen. Usually the results of such an attitude are unfortunate, but it is a characteristic premise of a nation at the zenith of its power. We frequently find the metaphor used in Victorian times.

Even the popular name given these English adventurers, *sea dogs*, has the virtue of reluctant admiration attached to it (dogs are dependably hard-working and faithful creatures). The most moral man may have been forced to concede, "Well, say what you will, these pirates did save England." The general opinion was that it was in Elizabethan times that the great traditions of English seamanship were founded. If it was Henry VIII (or Alfred) who started the English navy, it was the likes of the Drakes and Hawkinses who began the genius of the individual English sailor. Commander Robinson attributed the defeat of the Spanish fleet to the "foresight and enterprise of the English naval commanders," achieved with the help of shamefully underpaid, half-starved, and ill-supplied seamen. But the shameful conditions made the naval skill even more admirable, and they thus reinforce the myth of English seamanship. Vice Admiral Bedford called Drake the founder of a "system" of seamanship: it was Drake who taught English sailors that the proper way to fight an enemy was not to wait to be attacked but to pursue him to his own coast, a lesson which has borne good fruit ever since and "remains as true today as it was three hundred years ago."[13] It has certainly become an axiom of good strategy. One thinks, for example, of Nelson's oft-quoted phrase, "Engage the enemy more closely," a principle on which he acted all of his life.

According to the "system," the English seaman also did not wait to be ordered into battle but eagerly sought out the foe on his own. Again and again Drake requested permission from his reluctant sovereign to chase the Spanish into their home ports, chafing at the restrictions of her constant refusals. One author's imagery is significant: the "Nelson spirit was in Drake, and prompted him at times 'to turn the blind eye' to orders."[14] Drake's was not the diplomatic game of watch-and-wait but the straightforward, "manly" role of direct confrontation. His courage was so fantastic as to border on reckless insanity, and yet it was a kind of proof of the moral worth of his behavior that he should seem to lead such a charmed life. According to Froude, these English sea dogs, though proud and bold, were not heartless. "Drake never hurt a man if he could help it" (Froude claimed) and is often described as avenging the life of a child or the wrongs of a helpless man.[15]

Virtually all of the accounts of the Armada repeated the famous story of Drake and Lord Howard playing bowls on the lawns of Plymouth while waiting for the enemy. When word was brought to them that the Spanish fleet had been sighted in the English Channel, Drake was supposed to have said, "There is plenty of time in which to finish the game," or alternatively, "Let us play out our match. There will be plenty of time to win the game and beat the Spaniards too" (the exact phrasing varies). Even the words are fortuitous: the Victorians, at least the public-school class, made a fetish of games. Taking life as a game, that is, not taking it too seriously, became an important part of the English ethic. Just as the amateur was assumed to be more pure in heart than the professional, so the person who played life as a game was more heroic and admirable. By a kind of transference, Drake's attitude toward the Spanish also suggested a game.

Whether or not apocryphal, it is a fine tale, illustrating the cool courage and devil-may-care attitude of the English seaman whose contempt for the enemy was so great that he could not be bothered to interrupt his recreation. One writer, quoting the story, concluded with the moral, "These were stirring times, and the men who served Queen Elizabeth were worthy of the name of Englishmen." Commander Low's popular *Her Majesty's Navy* also related the anecdote of the bowling game, conceding that while the story may not have been, strictly speaking, historically true, it was as the Italians say, "*ben trovato.*" The author even stressed that the incident was important because it seemed to epitomize a quality that was undoubtedly Drake's, namely, his bland imperturbability in the face of danger. Although he did not use the word, Low was describing the kind of experience that I am terming *myth*, whose function is to dramatize and persuade, not to relate historical fact. In a later book, Low seemed almost to reverse his conclusion, however, when he commented that after all Drake had no very high opinion of Spanish valor and seamanship and thus could easily afford to wait until his game was done[16] (Incidentally, in 1964 yet another book on the Armada was published, bearing the title *Time to Finish the Game.*)

An interesting difficulty arises in connection with this question of English attitudes toward the Spanish. A contempt for one's enemy is a fine cohesive element and a promoter of fighting morale, but if the Spanish were not contemptible but brave and valiant, the victory over them was then even more glorious. The dilemma was never really resolved. Some writers saw the foe one way; some the other. There was, for example, the famous incident of the fire ships, a particularly common feature of the children's literature. Drake had filled eight ships with incendiary material and explosives, lit them, and sent them silently down into the midst of the Spanish fleet as it lay anchored in the harbor of Calais. It makes a dramatic story. The Spanish apparently had been expecting such a tactic, but they panicked, slipped their cables, and made for open sea. The fire ships did little more than psychological damage, but the incident delighted the English and served to increase their scorn of their enemy. Victorian writers tended to play it up or down, according to their estimate of Spanish valor.

Similarly, there was the incident of the Spanish captain, Don Pedro de Valdez of the *Capitana*, one of the finest ships in the fleet. Don Pedro was an able and courageous commander; but when his ship was badly crippled by gunfire, the Duke of Medina Sidonia anxiously ordered her abandoned to the English. Froude's account left no doubt that he thought this action cowardly and typical of the Spanish mind; "scandalous poltroonery," he called it.[17]

We find a similar attitude toward the Spanish character in Charles Kingsley, whose novel *Westward Ho!* concerned the voyages and life of Sir Amyas Leigh, Elizabethan adventurer. The fire ship incident produced "disgraceful panic" and the Spanish ships scattered like "truant sheep" and "stragglers." Leigh, in a raging desire to avenge a wrong to his brother, attempted to engage Don Guzman and his ship the *Santa Caterina*. The sense of the personal commitment to a fight; which is individual but also universal in its implications, is overwhelming. Lightning strikes Leigh, blinding him at the same time he kills his opponent, and the storm shatters the Spanish ship. Leigh is punished by God for overweening pride, but the Spaniard is punished, too. It is a very Victorian moral.[18]

❊   ❊   ❊

In trying to judge the significance of the Armada story, we find these various threads weaving a common theme. Victorian England saw the battle of the Armada as representing the beginning of English greatness based on impregnability reinforced with a new-found national skill at seamanship. The English found ironically amusing the term "invincible," which had been applied to Philip's fleet before the battle. That it had been not the Spanish but the English who had been invincible assumed a universal as well as historic truth. An interesting thing about the Armada myth, of course, is that the Victorian confidence in England's island security could only have taken on the force it had with the weight of three hundred years of proof. Never since 1588 had any would-be invader come so close to England's shores with an occupation force of troops on board. Even Napoleon, after all, never set sail, thanks to Nelson. Charles Dickens's famous *Child's History of England* described the defeat succinctly in the following words: "So ended this great attempt to invade and conquer England. And I think it will be a long time before any other invincible fleet coming to England with the same object will fare much better than the Spanish Armada."[19]

In another children's tale, Lady Callcott's *Little Arthur's History of England*, the Spanish king becomes a naughty child whose nanny had unsuccessfully warned him against playing with fire: "Philip must have been very sorry that he began to make war against England, for the war lasted as long as he lived, and every year the English admirals used to take a good many of his ships." Such bald moralizing might have been suitable for children, but the grownups' lessons were apt to be more disguised, though no less self-assured. Many writers saw the Armada as marking the beginning of the period in which England was queen of the sea, not only by might but by right. Some saw the Armada as the curtain raiser for the glorious saga of the British navy, and others as proof that England's liberties were best defended by a strong fleet. For Commander Robinson the lesson of the Armada was that Britain's shores were inviolate so long as her fleet was efficient. "As it is now, so it was then: the invasion of the country, thanks to the silver streak, is an impossibility so long as England maintains a sufficient force in the Channel to beat the enemy." And for Vice Admiral Bedford the proper place to fight England's enemies was on the sea, a principle that remained "as true today as it was three hundred years ago."[20]

The Armada story was also proof of God's favor. The implication that the Almighty had had a hand in the battle was paradoxically both pleasing and galling to the English sensibility. Froude described the English of the sixteenth century as believing that the defeat and destruction of the Spanish Armada was a declaration of the Almighty's faith in the causes of their country and the Protestant religion. But there was also, as we have noted, a parallel belief that ascribed the victory to English skill and English spirit. For example, the author of a letter to the *Pall Mall Gazette* on the occasion of the Nelson centennial in 1905 objected strenuously to the implication in the *Gazette's* editorial that the victory over the Armada was not due to human hands alone. The writer contended that it was not the Protestant wind but the defeat off Gravelines at the hands of Drake that curbed the power of Philip II and "established the basis of the British Empire."[21] Well, one cannot have it both ways; either God or the

English won the day. And yet in some senses one can have it both ways. If it was English skill that won the battle, this redounded to English credit. If God was responsible, this too redounded to English credit, because God favors the virtuous. Such dexterity with cause and effect illustrates another important use of myth: it can create a happy, or at least satisfactory, outcome from any event.

Curiously, the tercentenary of the Armada attracted very little attention from the British public. One exception to this rule was the *Illustrated London News*, which published two consecutive issues in July 1888, commemorating the anniversary. The town of Plymouth held a competition for a design for a suitable memorial, and Herbert A. Gribble (architect of the Brompton Oratory) won. The newspaper called his design "bold in its conception and treatment, symbolical in its character, eminently patriotic in spirit, and highly effective as a work of art." The winning design was a thirty-five-foot memorial with Britannia on top, trident in one hand, sword in the other. On the shaft of the pillar were medallion heads of Howard, Drake, Hawkins, Raleigh, and others. The base had the inscription He Blew with His Wind and They Were Scattered. On each side of the pillar was a statue, representing, respectively, Valor and Vigilance, and, running around the base, a series of shields representing the arms of the cities and towns that contributed to the defense of England in 1588. As a pictorial image of the Armada myth, it could not be more complete.

Generally speaking, however, there were very few commemorative articles and very little notice from the periodical press on the tercentenary. At first this might seem surprising, especially in light of the extremely self-congratulatory mood of Victorian nationalism. It is probable, however, that a point arrives in any national history and concomitant mythology where a legend has become so much a part of the common culture that it seems redundant to celebrate anniversaries. It will, for example, be interesting to see if much is made of the Nelson story in the year 2005.

I shall let Froude have the final word. He concluded his lecture on the Armada with a reiteration of his central theme and a summation of the moral of the story for Victorian England. In describing the results of the battle, he made the following comment, which is a fitting close to this chapter.

For the first time since Elizabeth's father broke the bonds of Rome, the English became a united nation, joined in loyal enthusiasm for the queen, and were satisfied that thenceforward no Italian priest should tithe or toll in her dominions. But all that, and all that went with it, the passing from

Spain to England of the scepter of the seas, must be left to other lectures. . . . My own theme has been the poor Protestant adventurers who fought through that perilous week in the English Channel and saved their country and their country's liberty.[22]

7

Heroism and the Myth of Nelson

Thine island loves thee well, thou famous man
The greatest sailor since the world began

Tennyson

Nelson was one of those great spirits to whom the world concedes an undisputed preeminence. As Shakespeare stands at the head of poets and Napoleon at the head of soldiers, so the immortal Nelson remains peerless among sailors.

Charles Rathbone Law, *Her Majesty's Navy*

PROBABLY NO FIGURE IS SO DURABLE IN THE NATIONAL MYTHOLOGY AS Horatio, Lord Nelson, hero of the battle of Trafalgar in 1805. To understand the longevity of his reputation, it is necessary to look at the social role of heroes.

The fascination with heroism was probably first apparent in the romantic worship of Napoleon early in the century. Certainly a reading of the popular literature of the Victorian period suggests that the English appetite for heroic exploits then was much larger than it would be today. In part this need for heroes might be attributed to an increasing suppression of individuality in an industrial society and a consequent yearning for a kind of substitute personal triumph in an admiration of the atypical. It is probably too facile a conclusion, however, since the conditions of crowded industrialism are even more apparent today than a century ago.

But the need for heroes was also a need for the embodiment of a moral ideal, especially in a society that was in transition from a dogmatic, traditional Christianity to a more relaxed emphasis on the "moral life." One should point out that for the Romantics and many Victorians the moral ideal was a personal one. The Napoleon worship

91

in the romantic age signaled a profound shift in moral viewpoint, however. Fascination with the man, the ego, the dominant personality of power and its mysterious attraction tended to supplant the traditional "moral" heroism of a St. George or a Beowulf, at least in serious literature. The need for moral certainty and religious security probably had the reverse effect on the general public: it made the need for a hero of clearly defined moral proportions all the more compelling. Thus even as the philosophers and major literary figures sensed the loss of the hero, the creatures of the popular culture venerated him all the more. In the popular culture, therefore, the tradition persists of a hero representing the best of the society, and to some extent, redeeming it with his virtuous action. Nelson at Trafalgar epitomized such redemption. As a century went on, this action could function increasingly outside the narrow frame of orthodox evangelicalism.

Finally, and perhaps most important, the need for heroes was an expression of a thirst for adventure. By reading about his national heroes the Victorian could thrill to vicarious participation in daring exploits of courage and bravery. The need for adventure, indeed, is central to the national heroic myth. The nineteenth-century Englishman admired the adventurers of his history—the Drakes and the Hawkinses—and took pride in their atypical and piratical behavior.

The word *hero* is in rather bad repute at present, suggesting as it does the glorification of qualities now considered rather antisocial since they are usually pictured in a military, or quasi-military, setting. But man has always created models for himself; and no society has been without its heroes, if we may define the word so broadly. The Victorian era was no exception, certainly, but there may have been an increase in the veneration for these models because of an ever more obvious contrast between the heroic life with its implications of freedom and individual initiative and the mechanical, drab, and circumscribed life of an overpopulated industrial nation, a contrast no longer considered unusual or worthy of remark today. It is very common for people in every age to express that they are at a loss to cope with the special problems they face, to feel that their society's abilities have decayed and that modern conditions are beyond their power. But those in nineteenth-century England thought they had more reason than most for feeling that way. Carlyle expressed his disgust in 1841: "I liken the common languid Times with their unbelief, distress, perplexity, with the languid doubting characters and embarrassed circumstances, impotently crumbling down into every worse distress towards final ruin;—all this I liken to dry dead fuel waiting for the lightning out of heaven that shall kindle it."¹ He asserted that in all the world's history it has been the great men who have provided the spark, "the lightning without which the fuel would never have burnt." Carlyle was speaking there in political terms, but the feeling, especially in later Victorian years, was not confined to the political arena. In fact, politics is a dangerous area to attempt heroic behavior because partisanship usually divides rather than unites a nation. Had Nelson survived and gone into politics, as Wellington did, for example, his luster might have tarnished. But the hero worship of Victorian England had many dimensions, from the popularity of the heroic epic to the lionizing of national figures who had won glory on the field of battle.

The emphasis on the military is important for three reasons. First, war provides a convenient stage for the demonstration of the heroic virtues, a stage made the more dramatic by the fact that emotions are heightened when the outcome is critical. Secondly, since the life of a nation often hangs in the balance, whatever virtues are displayed by the hero consequently become *national* virtues, and the hero becomes a kind of national image. Look, for example, at the way in which Churchill functioned as a national symbol in 1940: the embodiment of bulldog tenacity, stubborn courage, and defiance of overwhelming odds. Finally, the nineteenth century was apt to see war as a means of heroic action because of the shadows of revolution and Napoleon which hung over the whole age. To a large extent Napoleon represented the antithesis of Nelson, as revolution was the antithesis of liberal reform. Napoleon was the individual driven by evil will to power; revolution represented the unacceptably violent means to social change. Nelson was also driven by will, but under the necessary restraint of community with moral ends and moral definition.

Basic to the myth of heroism is the underlying belief that the attributes of the hero are human ones, that is, not beyond the reach of human perfectability. As Charles Kingsley pointed out in his famous essay on heroism, the word itself goes back to the Greek word for *godlike*, that is, *partaking of the divine*: "The hero by virtue of his kindred with the gods was always expected to be a better man than common men, as virtue was then understood." But Kingsley also thought it important to emphasize the model qualities of heroism, for if heroes do not become models for common men there would be no point to admiring them. One might just as well admire the gods. Kingsley went on, therefore, to argue that the capacity for heroism is in each one of us. It is "always

93

beautiful, always ennobling, and therefore always attractive to those whose hearts are not yet seared by the world or brutalized by self-indulgence."[2] Kingsley, writing a generation after Carlyle, carried the role of hero beyond that of the mere idol into a realm of educative values, and it seems characteristic of the later Victorian period that the models of Christian moral behavior were painted in human rather than divine terms. The hero, then, became the shining illustrative example, and as such he graced the pages of Samuel Smiles's improving works and, no less importantly for the development of myth, of the writers of juvenile literature.

What was involved in heroism? There were four qualities: courage, honor, modesty, and resourcefulness. It was essential to heroism that the hero have all four; possession of one or two did not lift him far enough above the ordinary to qualify for the title. Many were courageous, many were resourceful; it was only the unusual man who displayed these talents with integrity and becoming modesty.

Real courage, bravery, or pluck, as the English often termed it, meant boldness in the face of difficulty or danger, willingly confronting possible death. "True heroism must involve self-sacrifice," said Kingsley, emphasizing a genuine esthetic value: most people accepted self-sacrifice as "the highest form of moral beauty—the highest form and yet one possible to all." He considered it to be the highest because it involved the surrender of the ultimate gift, that of oneself. It is a gift, of course, in that it has to be a voluntary act. Mere slaughter of the innocent does not qualify, because it involves no human commitment; therefore the hero must choose to sacrifice himself in order that others may gain. Heroism must be "a work of supererogation, at least toward society and man: an act to which the hero or heroine is not bound by duty but which is above though not against duty."[3]

The second requisite for heroism was honor, by which was meant a whole host of traits including honesty, truth, dependability, and *character*. As we have mentioned, the Victorian was enthusiastic about character and considered it something to be instilled, like a series of Latin declensions, along with the pabulum of childhood. (Today the words *character* and *honor* have a kind of bogus quality. *Integrity* was not a word the Victorians used much, but it may better connote today what they meant by *honor*.)

The third heroic element was modesty. The hero was expected to be unassertive, self-deprecatory. He was to be not only passively unassertive but also actively loyal to his associates and his group, with the same kind of loyalty a team expects of its members. We have here, of course, something of a contradiction. The hero had in fact to stand out from his fellows, and yet he could not seem to want to stand out. His unusual quality had to come to him unsought. The welfare of the group was always to have primary importance. In fact, the conflict between the demands of self and the demands of society became *the* romantic dilemma from the early romantic writers to Sartre.

The last in the list of heroic attributes was resourcefulness. In order to be resourceful and self-reliant, the hero needed not only training but also a single heart. This virtue was linked to modesty, for it was only in forgetting the self that he could achieve the true greatness coming from devotion to the job at hand. Kingsley mentioned the values of simplicity in relation to heroism in this passage:

> Whatsoever is not simple; whatsoever is affected, boastful, willful, covetous, tarnishes, even destroys, the heroic character of a deed; because all these faults spring out of self. On the other hand, where ever you find a perfectly simple, frank, unconscious character, there you have the possibility, at least, of heroic action.[4]

The self-reliant hero had an inner spirit that courted solitude. The solitary soul was considered more admirable than the gregarious instinct, which was animal in origin. The soul was thought to be at its most spiritual when it was alone with itself. Only then could it commune with God and learn His purposes. The solitary element did not necessarily conflict with the ideal of loyalty to the group, for the group could consist of individuals who possessed an inner self-respect as well as an outward stance of conformity and loyalty.

All of these qualities would go for naught, however, if they were not exhibited in the proper spirit. A man—a hero—was expected to endure all hardship with a cheerful optimism. Courage, honor, modesty, and resourcefulness; these then were the heroic virtues. And none displayed them more thoroughly than Horatio, Lord Nelson, the embodiment of the nautical hero.

☼   ☼   ☼

It takes some time until any hero is permanently established in a national pantheon. Immediately following his death, there will be an outpouring of national grief and a sentimental glorification of the hero's exploits. Within a few years the immediate emotions will have diminished somewhat; biographers can be more critical,

95

the public more skeptical of virtue. At this point a reputation hovers between the ephemeral and the permanent. Provided the qualities of greatness and the significance of the battle are vital to the needs of the national myth, the hero will survive. Once beyond this critical point the hero's reputation seems assured, and he can safely be placed on the shelf of nationalism to lie undisturbed. Americans have only to look at George Washington, for example, to see how this process works. He was often vilified in his own lifetime; after his death his reputation soared. In the mid-nineteenth century he came to symbolize the individual qualities of the new nation and ultimately moved into an area beyond criticism. (Curiously, we cannot be absolutely positive of permanence, however. One would have said until very recently that Lincoln had also joined this group, but the present depreciation of his reputation by the black power movement may call his permanence into question.)

Nelson follows the same pattern. Immediately after the Battle of Trafalgar in which he lost his life, there was a predictable flood of national grief. There were biographies, biographical memoirs, and accounts of eyewitnesses to the battle. Most of this material was of poor quality and of secondary interest. The only outstanding item of the early period was Robert Southey's two-volume biography, published in 1813. A few minor accounts appeared at mid-century, along with the publication in 1844 of the dispatches and letters of Nelson in seven volumes.[5] Only a few other minor studies emerged in the eighty years following Trafalgar. By 1885 interest in Nelson had diminished considerably; he had not sunk into complete obscurity, although he now lived in a shadow, his heroism somewhat tarnished. At this point in his "afterlife" Nelson might have completely dropped out of sight. The critical period when Nelson became firmly entrenched in the national mythology were the years from 1885 to 1905, during which no fewer than ten major biographies appeared.

This surge of interest in the nautical hero suggests some of the significant functions of heroic myth in the national self-consciousness, particularly in the late-Victorian period. England was at this time facing unprecedented economic, political, and diplomatic competition from other nations. Her supremacy on the seas was beginning to be challenged, and she needed at this time to reinforce her confidence in herself and in her dominions through a reexamination and reappreciation of those qualities that led to her greatness. Now the nation could turn to Nelson as a personification of the national virtue and to the navy as the symbol of national greatness. He was certainly courageous. His reckless daring had won him renown again and again in his own lifetime. He had lost his right arm in the battle of Teneriffe at the age of thirty-eight, and the stories of his bravery and courage in the face of incredible pain through the amputation were legion. His last hours, lying on the lower deck of the *Victory*, suffering agony from a broken back, form a picture as familiar to the English schoolchild as Washington's cherry tree is to Americans. In commenting on Nelson's attitude toward the loss of his arm, Lieut. Charles Rathbone Low tells the story of Nelson's audience with the king, who had expressed sympathy for Nelson's wound. The hero replied, "May it please Your Majesty, I can never think [it] a loss which the performance of duty has occasioned, and so long as I have a foot to stand on I will combat for my king and country."[6]

A twentieth-century audience, contemptuous and suspicious of altruism and self-sacrifice, might look at such behavior and talk of death wishes, or at least see it as embarrassingly corny. The Victorians took a simpler view: for them self-sacrifice was courageous and ennobling; they found no hidden or sinister motives behind a desire to combat for king and country. Whether or not we can today accept such behavior as "real," we must acknowledge that many generations thought it was real, and their thinking so made it an operating reality.

Nelson's personality had other heroic qualities, too. For the Victorian public the hero had to be distinguished by a kind of morality that represented an ultimate distillation of the best in the national character. As moral prototype, Nelson was thoroughly so distinguished. His life was full of improving words and deeds for the instruction of the young. As I have mentioned, *character* was never very carefully defined by Victorian moralists, but it was clear to them who possessed it. A newspaper summed up Nelson's leadership abilities: "Personal character is in the last resort everything." Character involved personal integrity, but it also required a certain above-average generosity and humanity towards one's fellow man, even if he happened to be your enemy in battle. A writer of boys' adventure stories thought that this generosity of spirit was a major telling point of Nelson's character. He remarked that the British stood ready during the battle of Trafalgar to put out the fires on the French ships that had been caused by the British guns, "thus beautifully illustrating Nelson's prayer, 'that the British might be distinguished by humanity in victory.' " The author felt it important

97

to stress this element of magnanimous humanity because the greatest danger with heroes was that they should seem inhuman or superhuman in their greatness. Nelson was not such a one (compare him with Drake, for example, who was always described as careful of his men's welfare, a necessary ingredient in the myths of leadership.)[7]

From the point of view of the moralist, Nelson's life was fortunate in that it constantly illuminated that favorite Victorian watchword, *duty*. There was an intense moral ethic associated with this word. It is far too easy today for us to sneer at a society whose concept of duty seems to have involved a totally unwarranted interference in the lives of others, whether it was the white man's burden of the empire or the instruction of the poor at home. But whether or not we approve of the overt results of such action, the fact remains that much of the muscular Christianity of the nineteenth century was informed by a real concern to help others and by a profoundly sincere belief that it was every man's obligation (indeed, his *duty*) to help his fellowman. Duty was not something that could be put on and off like a coat at the convenience of the wearer; it was, rather, a lifelong obligation whose performance necessitated self-sacrifice and dedication.

There is probably no word more closely associated with Nelson than *duty*. Again and again, almost ad nauseam, the writers quoted his final words: "I have done my duty. I praise God for it." Or, alternatively, "Thank God I have done my duty." These words occasioned Commander Low's exclamation, "What nobler expression—and well justified by his life's history—could come from the lips of a dying man!"[8] It would be hard indeed to suspect that these dying words were anything but genuine on Nelson's part, since he himself had become, by the time of his death, as much a believer in his own growing legend as anyone else. But even if he were consciously speaking for posterity, the effect on the development of the Nelson myth would be the same. His famous Trafalgar signal, England Expects that Every Man Will Do His Duty, hoisted from the flagship *Victory* before the final battle, became engraved on the hearts of every English school child, many of whom, no doubt, committed to memory the signal flags that sent the message. The flag-signal order is often found as a decorative design on the endpapers of boys' books about the sea. Many biographers mention the story, perhaps apocryphal, of the hoisting of this signal. Apparently Nelson had first requested that the message begin with Nelson Expects but was persuaded to change it because there was a single flag for

England, and the word *Nelson* would have had to be spelled out. Far from detracting from his image, the anecdote enhances it, suggesting implicitly that England and Nelson were somehow synonymous.

By the time of the Nelson centennial the phrase, sometimes shortened to England Expects, could stand for the whole moral imperative associated with the national self-image. As the *Daily Mail* stated in 1905, "Duty was the watchword of Nelson's public life. At every turn the thought of it rises in his mind." The newspaper warned that this phrase had been no mere lip service to some vague ideal but a fixed and definite resolution in Nelson's mind, almost a determination on self-sacrifice for this concept. The lesson was clear: what Nelson could do, all should aspire to. The author of a boys' life of Nelson was just as emphatic: "Duty was the supreme law of his professional career. . . . For him, as for Wellington, duty was the one consideration about which debate was impossible, delay a dishonour, and denial the last and worst of treacheries." Southey's description of Nelson as having "served his country with all his heart and with all his soul and with all his strength" was frequently quoted by subsequent biographers as epitomizing the Nelson contribution. One writer of children's stories highlights this instructive and patriotic image, urging it as a good model to follow.[9]

The perfect hero was modest and self-denying, preferring to think of others before himself. Nelson's skill with his subordinates was mentioned again and again. He inspired and led his men and was very popular with them, as one writer put it, not because he pandered to their weaknesses and not by tolerating neglect of duty, but by showing care for their needs and by showing confidence in their desire to do their very best. The implication was clear: it takes real heroism to inspire courage and bravery in others. Professor J. K. Laughton, in a popular pamphlet, "The Story of Trafalgar," wrote of the remarkable good fellowship that existed between Nelson and his subordinates: "Probably no officer in Nelson's position has ever possessed to the same extent the power of winning the confidence and the love of those he commanded. Service under Nelson was a service of love as much as of duty."[10]

The contrast between the fellowship that existed in the navy and that was apparently lacking in the army reflected a common English belief. Nelson also had a very poor opinion of soldiers and was quite prejudiced against the army. He once wrote to his wife, "Armies go so slowly that seamen think they never mean to get forward." He considered the sailor the highest type of man, and he had the most unbounded confidence in his own men, perhaps a self-fulfilling proposition. It is well documented that Nelson's men, from his captains down to the lowliest cabin boy, behaved far better under fire and were more disciplined than almost any other crew of British sailors. This may have been attributable to his great care for their abilities and needs. But it is also true that this is the way in which myth inspires and persuades. In his own time, he was thought to be the best of leaders: the result of such belief would be not only that the leader himself is motivated to fulfill the prediction, but also that those led would believe themselves fortunate. A children's book, *In the Days of Nelson*, is the story of a boy who went to sea, served under Nelson, and returned to his home to claim his rightful inheritance stolen from him by a wicked uncle. In the end he became a midshipman on Nelson's ship as a reward for his heroism in rescuing a crewman in the battle. As one newspaper commented, Nelson was always considerate of his men and won all their hearts. He would see what was best in a man and expect him to act up to it.[11]

The care and feeding of a heroic reputation requires a great deal of attention to romantic detail, and the biographers did not have to search far for material with which to enliven their task. For example, almost all of them mention or quote the story of the time Nelson received his mortal wound on the deck of the *Victory*. As he was removed to await the surgeon's attention, he noticed that the tiller ropes were shot away. He stayed his porters long enough to give the orders for the ropes' replacement. Although a dying man, he was the careful seaman to the last. His care for his men persisted to the last: when he was carried below to the makeshift dispensary on the orlop deck of the *Victory*, he asked that the attendants cover his wounds so that the other wounded sailors might not be overcome with dismay at the sight of their commander. He also insisted that the doctors deal with the seriously wounded men before they turn their attention to him.

The story of Nelson's final hours was so well known that it scarcely needed retelling, but no biographer could resist the lessons. Even the way in which he received his fatal wound seemed appropriately heroic in outline and behavior. It was Nelson's custom to walk the quarterdeck of the flagship during a battle dressed in complete admiral's regalia with his medals shining on his chest. He was thus in full view of the enemy, whose ships were usually near enough for French marksmen to pick off the English sailors. When his subordinates remonstrated with him that he made an elegant and conspicuous target, Nelson stated simply that he preferred to stand as an ex-

100

ample of honor than to hide in disguise. Whatever the prudent might think of such acts, the Victorians clearly admired not only the bravery but also the honesty of the position. The proper place for an admiral to direct a battle was on the quarterdeck, and only a coward would pretend to be a common sailor in order to avoid an enemy bullet!

For three hours the wounded Nelson lay in his bunk below, suffering extreme thirst and excruciating pain. Again and again he asked for news of the battle and how many of the enemy were taken. His friend Captain Hardy replied that it was impossible to see distinctly, but he thought that fourteen or fifteen ships had been captured at a minimum. "That's well," cried Nelson, "but I had bargained for twenty."[12] Almost his final words to Hardy were an order to anchor the fleet so that the English ships should not be scattered at sea during the night.

Nelson's last order thus nicely illustrates another quality—his superb seamanship. Professor Laughton, an expert naval historian, attributed the success not only of Trafalgar but also of Nelson's other exploits to his daring disregard for conventions of strategy. Nelson had great self-confidence and was not afraid to try new methods or tactics. Admiral Colomb, a well-respected officer in his own time, greatly admired what he described as Nelson's combination of "fire and ice." He called Nelson a more "specially inspired being than any great man of modern times," ascribing the genius to his originality.[13] Where other commanders fell back on precedent, Nelson forged ahead with daring innovations. His "new ideas" were particularly inspired and successful at the Battle of Egypt, where (it is generally agreed) the victory would probably have been a defeat had a more conventional attack been tried. Nelson apparently took full responsibility for this decision, but he kept his captains informed of his plans. He did not ask their advice in advance but trusted them to know the correct responses to any contingency which might have arisen during the battle, thus demonstrating the virtues of self-reliance and resourcefulness while also maintaining the proper respect for the skills of his subordinates. Even the popular writers, who knew less than the experts of the technical aspects of Nelson's seamanship, were quick to praise his "marvelous insight," "prompt vigor," and "splendid moral courage," calling him a man who made his own opportunities.[14]

When dealing with a hero, a biographer's major problem is how to treat the hero's faults. With Nelson, the usual human failings were complicated by the existence of his mistress, "dear Lady Hamilton," as he almost invariably referred to her. In the Victorian period,

101

when sexual aberration was usually swept under the rug, it was very difficult for the biographers to cope with Nelson's love affair. Lady Hamilton was far too important in Nelson's life to ignore completely, but to acknowledge her role was to seriously besmirch a hero's reputation. It is interesting to see how each of the biographers dealt with this difficulty. One solution was to describe Nelson's wife as so disagreeable as to make Nelson's betrayal of her understandable, thus blackening Lady Nelson in order to brighten her husband. An example of this approach is Vice Admiral Colomb's biography, in which he described Lady Nelson as a very cool person, incapable of understanding her husband, someone who "seems never to have been in touch with Nelson's passionate nature." Colomb decided that if Nelson's wife had been all that she should have been, Nelson would never have fallen for Lady Hamilton.[15]

Another approach to the Nelson-Hamilton problem was to make Lady Hamilton herself the villainess of the piece. Many biographers, particularly the earlier ones, painted her as a seductress who led the hero astray. Poor Nelson was a man unfamiliar with the wiles of wicked women; he was so pure and upright that he failed to perceive the deceit of this woman and of her relationship with him. W. Clark Russell, a popular writer of sea stories, took this approach. He thought that Nelson was very much in love with his wife Fanny Nisbet, and Russell strongly disapproved of Lady Hamilton. Trying to refute the idea that Nelson was stricken with love the first time he saw her, Russell doubted that the fascination of "purely sensuous charms can ever wholly dominate the neutralizing element of vulgarity in a woman." Emma Hamilton had in fact been first a servant (and therefore of low-class origins), and then the mistress to three men before Nelson. She was thus "no better than she should be," and could be dismissed as relatively unimportant.[16]

Professor Laughton took a similar path. He condemned Lady Hamilton, describing her as "licentious" and also, for good measure, as "ignorant of the distinction between truth and falsehood." We thus cannot trust what she said and must discount much of the content of the stories she spread about herself and Nelson after his death. But Laughton's treatment of Nelson's role in the love affair is revealing. By a circuitous logic he implied that Nelson's love for Lady Hamilton simply illustrated that even great men can have an occasional weakness. Thus, a hero can be made to seem more manly and great because he occasionally is human enough to be led astray by an evil person! We are therefore invited to pity and sympathize with Nelson but scarcely to condemn him, particularly when, as Laughton made abundantly clear, the lady did not even really love him but was only out to get what she could from him. In a similar way Russell described Emma Hamilton as a "vain, lowborn, unprincipled woman" and saw Nelson's connection with her as a deplorable but understandable fault.[17] The biographers thus tried to explain away a fault, then tried to attribute it to someone else, and finally, when the facts could not be blinked, suggested that the existence of the fault was one of those minor flaws in spite of which the man rose into greatness.

There was also the problem of Nelson's illegitimate daughter, Horatia. Clearly she was the child of this love affair between Nelson and Lady Hamilton, but many writers spent an inordinate amount of time trying to demonstrate either that she was not Nelson's child or that she was not Lady Hamilton's child. The contemporary evidence is overwhelming, however. Although the pair was discreet, Nelson never tried to deny that Horatia was his daughter; he was extremely proud and fond of her, and he mentioned her in his final letter. Just before the battle of Trafalgar, fearing that he might not survive, he wrote a document requesting the government to support Lady Hamilton and Horatia. The government did not undertake this obligation, and Lady Hamilton's "claims" remained unrecognized. According to Russell, however, she should have been in no financial difficulty at all since she had about £1500 annually from both Nelson's and Sir William Hamilton's estates; but her extravagance plunged her into debt, and (evil woman that she was) her "vanity and shiftlessness disgusted those who had been willing to assist her." Thus she got only what she deserved.[18]

The other major difficulty facing biographers was Nelson's undeniable ambition and vanity. The battle of the Nile won Nelson a barony, but Sir John Jervis, commander of the fleet, had obtained an earldom as a result of the battle of St. Vincent in 1797. This inequality annoyed Nelson, and he made several remarks about his ill treatment at the hands of the government. Such an attitude might seem petty in a hero whose only care should have been for the greater concerns of victory and patriotism. But in another way it was appropriate for a man to resent being overlooked by the government because a keen sense of justice was also a heroic attribute. Commander Low described the situation this way: "Though Nelson throughout his life was only inspired by a sense of duty, he keenly felt the unworthy treatment to which he

103

had been subjected on this and former occasions, and openly expressed his indignation."[19]

Again, as with the difficulty in dealing with Emma, some of the biographers turned fault into virtue. In a centennial essay on Nelson, former prime minister Lord Rosebery remarked that a sense of having been ill used was a good index of popularity. One could never trust governments to do the right thing; thus the more an unworthy man was promoted ahead of the worthy one, the more sure one could be of the latter's virtue! Even if one conceded that Nelson was competitive, Rosebery thought that it was natural in a hero to be ambitious, and he described this ambition in Shakespeare's words, "But if it be a sin to covet honor, I am the most offending soul alive."[20]

Not all the biographers, however, would concede that Nelson was greedy for honor and glory or vain and ambitious. Some of them claimed that he was the most retiring of men and that he had been maligned by other writers who had manufactured the boast and bravado. According to Russell, the most conspicuous of Nelson's qualities was his modesty: "We may be quite sure that he said but very little of what has been put into his mouth." While it is probably true that many of the hero's conversations and comments were invented, sufficient written material does exist to document the vanity and ambition. The writers were certainly on safer ground, historically speaking, if they adhered to the pattern of either painting fault as virtue or else claiming that a weakness or two makes a hero human.[21]

In order to understand the security and power of the Nelson myth we must look at his final victory. The writers were unanimous in saying that Trafalgar was among the most significant events not only in naval history but in all of English history. To Trafalgar alone is attributed the glory of the final defeat of Napoleon. For one writer no great battle ever had such great consequences: as a result of Trafalgar the sea power of France and Spain vanished and "Britannia arose, in very truth, mistress of the seas." Another described the intention of the French as nothing less than the invasion of Britain, arguing that without Trafalgar's destruction of the French fleet Britain would surely have succumbed. Laughton agreed, pointing out that Napoleon was so confident of victory that he had collected a hundred and fifty thousand men at Boulogne for the projected invasion. Trafalgar forever scotched these plans, having "shattered beyond recovery the naval power of France and Spain."[22]

But however important Trafalgar was from the strategic and military point of view, it became even more important as a symbol. Browning's poem "Home-Thoughts from the Sea" illustrates this:

> Bluish 'mid the burning water, full in face
>   Trafalgar lay;
> In the dimmest North-east distance dawned
>   Gibralter grand and gray;
> "Here and here did England help me: how can
>   I help England?"—say

And one rabidly patriotic minor civil servant, who wrote a book for school children called *The English Citizen: His Life and Duty*, described Trafalgar as having destroyed forever the arrogant power that threatened the liberty of civilization. For Laughton, Trafalgar represented the downfall of tyranny and oppression, the saving of Great Britain and the liberation of Europe.[23] The hero thus became the "redeemer" who designed and directed the battle. His final self-sacrifice conquered evil (Napoleon) and redeemed and saved society.

The battle was seen not only as an end but as a beginning: it marked the opening of the period in which Britain controlled the world's oceans. In Commander Low's words, "Henceforth our country remained the undisputed Mistress of the Seas." Finally Trafalgar also functioned not only as the vital naval victory, the symbol of Britain's preeminence, and the rescue from threat of invasion, but also as the symbol of the greatness to which English seamen could rise when called upon. Laughton expressed this very well when he wrote that the whole secret of "this wonderful victory" lay in the happy combination of tactical genius, skill, experience, fellowship, training, and good discipline. "But these qualities do not grow spontaneously: they require cultivation and development; they are the product of obedience, labor, and forethought, of unceasing energy, zeal, and devotion: and the encouragement to all these lies in the glorious and ever-living memory of TRAFALGAR."[24]

For the architect of the great victory, the function was a similar one. Not only was Nelson responsible for Trafalgar, he personified it. We see the culmination of this in the Trafalgar centennial celebration of 21 October 1905. Many new biographies were published, one of which had an interesting new twist: Nelson was treated fictionally as a naval hero of a contemporary English

105

war with an unnamed enemy. All the traditional elements were in the story: the duty signal, Nelson's wound, his final prayer, his death in the arms of his captain, Hardy, who says to him, "You die in the midst of the world's greatest triumph." "Do I, Hardy?" he smiles faintly. "God be praised!" These were his last words. Presumably by bringing the story up-to-date, the consequences of Trafalgar and heroism were made more vivid for the young reading public.[25]

Many newspapers and magazines devoted a whole issue to the centennial celebrations, and here the development of the myth is clearest. According to the *Manchester Guardian*, for example, the chief lessons of Nelson's life lay in the "intellectual and moral elements" that insured a victory: "He saw what was best in a man and expected him to act up to it. Self-sacrifice did more than anything to make men better than before, and it was also a great factor in building up nations." It was part of a larger Victorian myth that progress, success, and, of course, victory were achieved by things like self-sacrifice; mere items like materiel or numbers were not very significant. From the late Victorian period onward the seamanship and tactics associated with the old wooden sailing vessels were no longer particularly useful; but stress was always put on the breed of men needed to man the modern navy, a breed of men not less heroic and patriotic than those of a hundred years previous. As Russell wrote, "So long as the English sailor preserves his qualities, the name of Nelson must prove a note of magic. It will be these qualities which will, in turn, preserve the place of Britain."[26]

In his preface to the centennial issue of the *United Service Magazine*, Lord Rosebery wondered why Nelson stood in history not merely as a nautical hero but as the quintessential hero of Britain. True, Wellington might be considered almost as great for his military success, but Nelson had avoided politics whereas Wellington had not. Rosebery dwelt on "the fascinating incongruity of a warrior's soul being encased in so shriveled a shell" and on his chivalrous devotion to his officers, his manifest and surpassing patriotism, and his unwearied pertinacity. Rosebery concluded that one must look for the key to Nelson's greatness in the symbolic association of Nelson with the sea. It must be remembered, he remarked, "that the sea is the British element."[27]

*   *   *

How can we characterize the Nelson figure emerging as a myth? Although Nelson started as a ready-made hero in 1805 with a sufficient quantity of the remarkable to place him with the extraordinary, his reputation grew, especially in the last part of the century. A popular writer of 1885, discussing Nelson's vast reputation with the people of his own day, emphasized the love he inspired in the English public: "He was their Nelson; not the Nelson of the court or of the aristocracy, but the Nelson of the people of England." Nelson seems to have aroused this public love almost from the very beginning as the symbol of national greatness. One newspaper commented that Englishmen would always fight well because courage was "the incomparable response of brave men" to Nelson's personal magnetism.[28]

Both Nelson and Trafalgar thus became synonymous with British greatness, British daring, British domination of the seas, British courage, and British defiance of a strong foe. A boys' story of six English sailors who fought German submarines in the First World War has a battle chapter titled, significantly, "The Nelson Touch," and at one point the author remarks, "for it would seem that the spirit of Nelson were abroad that day, that he was watching, that he had touched those brave hearts with his spirit-finger and steeled them to even greater heroism." A similar work a few generations earlier exclaimed, "May we always have a Nelson in the hour of national need!" And a school history book, written "for all boys and girls who are interested in the story of Great Britain and her Empire" stressed the enduring significance of the hero: "You can see the *Victory* still moored in Portsmouth harbour, and can go into the little dark cabin in which Nelson died, happy in spite of mortal pain, because he lived long enough to hear of England's triumph."[29]

Nelson is probably secure in his place in the national myth so long as the English continue to associate their history with sea, and to admire courage, self-sacrifice, and a certain poignancy in the unnecessary but romantic quality of death. Nelson remains, as Rosebery called him, the greatest of heroes: "We can boast of no more unquestioned genius, no truer patriot, no soul more instinct with the sacred fire of higher ambition. . . . He is indeed unique." Nelson's example as an English sailor must "whilst there remains a British keel afloat, be as potent in all seafaring aspirations and resolutions as ever it was at any moment in his devoted and glorious life."[30]

Part 4

THE MYTHS OF THE NAVY

THE NAVY IS PERHAPS THE MOST VISIBLE SYMBOL IN THE VICTORIAN myths of the sea; it serves to bring into focus the myths of greatness, of destiny, and of moral purpose in the national life. In chapter 8 I examine the symbolic role of the navy and its position as defensive shield; chapter 9 deals with the way in which the naval administration met the challenges to Victorian supremacy on the seas.

8

The Navy as Symbol and Defense

What is more characteristically English than the Navy?

W. H. Davenport Adams, *England on the Sea*

In spite of what foreign liars may say . . . every right-thinking intelligent Briton knows that in the fullest sense of the word the motto of the British Navy is "Defence not Defiance."

Bullen, *Our Heritage of the Sea*

The Navy, whereupon, under the good Providence of God, the wealth, safety, and strength of the Kingdom chiefly depend.

Naval Discipline Act

"WHAT IS MORE CHARACTERISTICALLY ENGLISH THAN THE NAVY?" Clearly, to the Victorians, the answer was nothing. In this chapter I shall examine the navy first in its symbolic role: in association with empire, representing the freedom of the seas, and personifying moral force. Next I shall deal with naval supremacy and the navy in its defensive role. Finally, I shall examine the naval myths of the practice of war.

The need of a nation for visual symbols of its nationhood is commonplace. Robert Louis Stevenson thought that Britain's totem might be the sea, but more realistically speaking it was her empire and her navy which at the zenith of her power served as twin emblems of her pride in the latter part of the nineteenth century. Empire and navy were closely interlinked in many minds and, as we shall see, often interchangeable. The British took great pride in the sheer enormity of their empire. Maps of the world in nineteenth-century English textbooks and atlases show the British possessions as red in color. "Painting the map red" was a well-understood

111

cliché of late Victorian imperial expansion. To some extent Britain's power was considered to be but the natural organic outgrowth of certain inherent qualities of her race and her political position. To many other people the expansion of the empire in the nineteenth century was the direct result of Britain's clearly dominant role in shipping and commerce and of the concomitant need to protect this business and the business of Britain's merchants abroad. As the most highly evolved civilization, the British were naturally to be found in the far corners of the world expanding their trade, founding new nations abroad, and bringing the blessings of representative government to backward peoples.

Victorians were more preoccupied than we with the concept of the nation, complicated as it was for them by problems of definition, as we have seen. The attitudes varied from an extreme insularity of "little Englandism" to a vast, Rhodesian embrace of all English-speaking peoples into some kind of giant pan-British nation. Some writers took an aggressively social-Darwinist point of view, insisting that Britain's nationhood was an organism that needed to grow and be cultivated in order to survive. For example, Spenser Wilkinson, journalist and military expert, wrote in 1909 that Britain had neglected her "nationhood" and that this neglect had been the cause of Germany's catching up with Britain. He felt keenly the German threat to European peace and rather accurately predicted the eventual outcome, although he conceded Germany the right to build defenses for herself. Such a concession was more generous than the feeling of some nationalists who, as *The Globe* rather wryly remarked, carried the idea of naval supremacy to such lengths "that the foreigner's aspiration to the possession of a fleet appears to them in the light of a personal grievance." But these were significant patriotic complaints, since the naval competition of the late nineteenth century was to some extent a competition for the visual symbol of national greatness. If another nation built a fleet, it became not only a military challenge but a threat to national identity.[1]

Some of these superpatriots were extremely truculent in their attitude. A pamphlet written in 1912 for the Imperial Maritime League deplored both Germany's aggressiveness and Britain's weakness. According to the authors, Germany wanted trade, colonies, and glory, desires which threatened Britain's very existence. They also argued, in another pamphlet, that when a man loses the instinct of self-preservation, his life is unlikely to be long, and when a nation loses the same instinct, its independence will be similarly short. But if the navy remained strong, Britain could surge forward, increase her colonies, get fresh markets, and insure her predominance as a nation for at least another hundred years. In fact it would be a positive good for Britain to go to war; the self-sacrifice and energy needed to prosecute a war successfully would be crowned by a victory of monumental proportions, a victory that would have a moral as well as a physical quality: "Survival of the fittest means survival of the ethically best." What Britain needed was a revival of that "dying military spirit which God gave to our race that it might accomplish His will on earth"[2] (an attitude that perhaps explains some of the dislike of Britain felt by other nations).

The emphasis on a racial destiny for power, glory, and empire is typical of the myths of the navy. There was a close association of the navy with the empire; the navy was the source of, as well as the protector of, the power that won the empire. In John Ruskin's inaugural lecture, speaking of the destiny of Britain, he stressed the connection between empire and sea, urging Britain to found colonies as fast as possible in order that she have outposts of power across the globe. The citizens of these distant Englands would be as truly English as those at home, no more disenfranchised from their native land than the sailors of the fleet were. The comparison is a significant one, for he went on to call the colonies "fastened fleets" and "motionless navies." Each member of the crew must be as subject to his captains and officers as is any Jack Tar, casting themselves, if necessary, "into the cannonmouths for love of England." We can easily reverse Ruskin's metaphor: if the colonies could be called fastened fleets, the navy could as easily be considered a moving colony, for the fleet symbolized much of the grandeur and purpose of the late-Victorian imperialists in their justification of expansion. The colonist in Ruskin's image was a seaman devoted to the British cause; here the seaman is a colonist searching the vast trackless wilderness for the greater glory of England, carrying with him his superior civilization and his interest in the arts of good government. "God-given, surely, is this mighty Empire into the hands of the Anglo-Saxon Race to be used for God and for the good of Man," exclaimed one writer.[3]

The idea that the British had a natural aptitude for colonization was a common one. A school textbook, written by a man who specialized in nautical adventure stories for children, emphasized that the only colonies of any importance were the ones which belonged to Great Britain. Other peoples could never quite get the knack of empire: "The French, however, unlike the British, are not natural colonists. They make good traders and explorers, but are always eager to return to France." He echoed Ruskin's idea that the colonies were, indeed, little Britains, not colonies in the dependent, inferior sense of other empires. The sea became, here, not an incidental path over which one travelled, but an integral part of the whole. If the sea were English, there must be no essential distinction, then, between home and colony. The *Naval and Military Magazine* published a poem in July 1897 (at the height of the Jubilee celebrations) called "A Song of Imperial Unity" which closes with this chorus:

> Sons of Britannia, in love's federation,
>   Drawn, as her sea mists are drawn, by the Sun;
> Offering the Homeland the heart's best oblation,
> From Earth's farthest corner with proud salutation,
>   Muster in myriads—as One![4]

This image of Grea*t*er Britain was most popular during the height of the interest in Imperial Federation in the eighties and nineties, but it clearly dated back to Ruskin at least (1870), and we find it cropping up later as well. A historian who was brought up in the late-Victorian period (although writing after the First World War) repeated this idea of small Britains afloat around the globe. He called the British empire "practically all insular," as though the colonies were satellites which had incidentally broken off from the matrix island but were still made of the same material. Such a distinction in empires was often cited as the source of Britain's greatness and endurance in the imperial realm. I shall return to this idea later.[5]

Other phrases used to describe the empire are significant. Mowat called it a "water empire," and Sir Charles Dilke and Spenser Wilkinson, the Liberal statesman and the popular journalist who together wrote the influential book *Imperial Defence*, called the British empire the "possession of sea." From the sea the colonies, "like ourselves, derive their nourishment and their strength." They went on to argue that if the sea froze or dried up the empire would perish—a psychologically interesting anxiety.[6]

The mythic identification of the empire with the navy rather than with the sea was not usually so explicit as Ruskin made it, although his phrase "motionless navies" was quoted so often that it became trite. Much more usual, of course, was the association of the navy as the link between colony and home, the lifeline of the empire. The picture of the navy as the major defense of the outer limbs of the body politic was particularly vivid when writers discussed India, which was often referred to as the "Jewel of the Crown." The British felt vulnerable with respect to India, partly because the memory of the Mutiny of 1857 was still fresh in some minds, and partly because it was the largest single colony with a non-British population. Charles Rathbone Low, who had served with the Indian navy, wrote in 1878 of the importance of the navy to the "safe-keeping of the seaboard of our Eastern possessions." Dilke and Wilkinson, some twenty years later, made a similar point, stressing the need to protect the work of "peace and good government which has been undertaken in India" and the need to retain command of the seas as the essential ingredient in the maintenance of the empire.[7]

Since Britain was an island, if she cared to have an empire at all she had to have naval communication with that empire, and it had to be not only a strong communication, it had to be superior to all other powers. This point was insisted upon time and time again, and it bears some examination. In an article for the *Navy League Annual*, the Right Honorable, the Earl of Meath, wrote, "No sane man . . . can doubt that an Empire divided like ours is by vast expanses of ocean, can alone maintain its existence by retaining the undisputed command of the sea."[8] That Britain should have good sea communications is obvious, but why she needed undisputed command is more obscure. Probably the answer is to be found in a fear that the jealousy of other nations was so overwhelming that if Britain were not vastly superior, she would immediately be devoured by the ravening wolves of international competition. Perhaps one expects such talk from professional alarmists—members of the Navy League, government officials or civil servants whose care and interest is naval defense—but the universality of the opinions as reflected in the newspapers leaves little doubt that this was a popular feeling. The need for physical superiority reflected a need for acknowledgment of an internal superiority; Britain would like other nations to reinforce her sense of position—the acceptance of superior strength (as measured in numbers of ships) would be one indication that they did so. It is not therefore terribly surprising that with such a psychology and an almost paranoid view of the rest of the world, the British public would fasten onto something like naval superiority as essential to their very existence and assume that they would never abandon the command of the seas without great struggle.

In the naval mythology, therefore, the navy stood for the empire, for the communications between the members of the empire, and for the shield which guarded Greater Britain. It also symbolized the ideals of British nationalism that emerge so consistently from the patriotic literature of the time. John Leland, author of numerous works on naval history, concluded his pamphlet, *The Achievement of the British Navy in the World War*, with a chapter entitled "What the British Navy Is and What It Fights For." According to Leyland, the freedom of the Englishman, his most cherished possession, was guaranteed to him by sea power. The German saw this freedom as undisciplined weakness, whereas the so-called freedom of the German, guaranteed to him only by the military strength of an autocracy, was not a real freedom but a species of feudal or medieval dependence. Thus the German was a pitiable object, deceived by his nation into thinking himself free when actually he was but a modern version of a serf. Leyland believed there was a fundamental antithesis between the ideals of the German and the English nations, since the German accepted this condition as good while the Englishman considered it deplorable. (It is significant that the author assumed that naval power was "modern" and "freedom loving," where other kinds of military power were old-fashioned and "medieval.")

But the freedom of the Englishman was not even a selfish possession since the navy also guaranteed to every other nation not internal freedom, which would be beyond its powers, but at least the very real freedom of the seas. This freedom was historically a voluntary gift of the navy, first to the British Empire, and then to the rest of the world. The other nations of the world had only to look at the depredations on innocent, neutral shipping in wartime to realize how important such a gift was to international peace and harmony. Leyland concluded his book with the comment that the command of the sea which the navy exercised "is the panoply of freedom and liberty throughout the world."[9]

In a chapter titled "Navies and Armies: What the British Navy Has Done for the World," a similar book argued that naval and military power were very different from each other. The latter could be an instrument of tyranny; navalism could not. The author contended emphatically that naval strength could not enslave and subjugate people against their will. "Has anyone yet heard of a Nero, a Caesar, a Napoleon of the seas?" No, he has not. While history teems with examples of populations trodden under foot by hostile armies, there are no examples of naval tyranny. It is impossible: a navy cannot interfere with the internal economy of any state, with its laws or customs, its religion or government; it cannot overrun cities, it cannot destroy, it cannot climb mountains, occupy towns, or enslave peoples. The records of sea power in history show that quite to the contrary navies have often curbed a tyrant's designs and set a limit to a destructive career. "Sea power is an arresting and defensive, military power always an aggressive force."[10]

The reader may want to discount much of this sentiment as simply patriotic wartime fervor, but I think it would be mistaken to do so. A nation's myths about itself are expressed most baldly under the pressure of wartime emotion; war allows people to say what they really feel, uninhibited by the canons of modesty or social politeness. It might be argued, indeed, that a national myth is revealed at its most naked in times of stress.

We find some of the same feelings at an earlier date. There was a huge Naval Review in 1897, some of it open to the public. The Navy League published a helpful guide to the show complete with descriptions of all the ships, pictures for easy identification, and articles by various naval experts. Sir Edward Reed, an eminent naval architect, commented in the guide on the purpose of the navy, "We do not build our war fleets for the purpose of attacking anyone," he wrote, "for lowering the name or fame of any nation, or for subjecting any free and happy people to our rule. What we build . . . for is to maintain the freedom of the high seas."[11]

Freedom of the seas meant different things to different people. It is doubtful if other nations all accepted the British definition; Britain and the United States once had a serious disagreement over the subject. Spenser Wilkinson expressed what was for many Victorians the proper way to look at the phrase. Freedom of the seas, he wrote, is a "condition of law and order over all the navigable salt water." This was published in 1920, but it was as much a prewar as a postwar attitude. Never before in history, Wilkinson claimed, except for a brief period of the Roman Empire on the Mediterranean Sea, had the seven seas been so free as they had been in the two or three generations before the First World War, an achievement due solely to the presence of the British navy.[12]

Britain as guarantor of freedom of the seas was not simply a passive symbol but an active force. The Victorian was fond of pointing out historical instances of how seriously the navy took its self-

117

assigned task. One historian called it "one of the great conserving forces of the nineteenth century," whose main concerns were "defense, communications, the slave trade, and general helpfulness." There was no sea in the world (with the exceptions of the Black and Caspian, which could be dismissed as backwater and unimportant) that the British navy did not patrol and guard. The navy had rid the waters of piracy and worked hard to eliminate the internationally banned slave trade, a nefarious practice not far removed from piracy. This was not a single action but a long, determined, and continuing struggle. Much of the credit for the disappearance from the high seas of these twin evils could be given to the British navy.[13]

In fact, the issue of the slave trade was one of the most frequently cited instances of the high-minded work of the navy. The memoir of a late-Victorian admiral, who had considerable experience both at sea and at the admiralty, reflected this concern as a moral one. He emphasized that the ships involved in suppressing the slave trade had to struggle with a very "trying and monotonous service, day after day, month after month, and our vessels were then kept at it for two and sometimes three years without change." He stated without rancor but with considerable satisfaction that he never encountered a single vessel of any other nation engaged in this useful work. "It was said at one time that the British Navy interfered with the freedom of the seas. This stopping of an infamous traffic is the only instance in my recollection that might be quoted against us, and if it was wrong we must accept the blame." What is striking here, however, is the emphasis upon the navy as "moral instrument"; the myth of defender of right and justice, irrespective of persons or national sovereignties, is strong. Lest the reader think this attitude is peculiar to the English or to the nineteenth century, one could point to any major diplomatic argument of the last forty years for similar examples. While Admiral Eardley-Wilmot was on duty in the Middle East, he frequently gave refuge to runaway slaves who were then sent to the city of Aden to be trained and educated and freed. It was not surprising that there should be some objection to the practice from foreign nations.[14]

Up to the time of the American Civil War, of course, there was considerable market for slaves both in the southern states and in Spanish America. It was, apparently, a toss-up as to which of the two areas of trade—the American or the Arabian—was the more horrifying. The Baltimore clippers used in the American trade were fast and well manned and extremely clever at avoiding pursuit.

Their captains would not infrequently throw their human cargoes overboard to escape detection, or they would sail in squadrons, with a single ship detached as decoy when necessary. The conditions on the Arab *dhows* engaged in trade along the east coast of Africa were no better than on the notorious American slavers.

Frank Bullen, author of a number of sketches and tales about the sea, told a story of sailing in the Indian Ocean, where he saw an Arab slave ship. "Fervently I hoped that some of my countrymen were lying hidden near enough to stop those incarnate devils on their infernal errand." As he scanned the horizon he glimpsed a British "guardship" with five hundred "eager fellows on board ready to take any risk to stop such villainous craft as was now befouling the seascape." He ignited a rocket from his own vessel to inform the British of the presence of the slaver, then watched through his binoculars as the steam launch arrived to cut off the Arab's escape. It was nip and tuck for a few moments, but ultimately the British ship captured the other, and Bullen's heart leaped up as he saw the "red and white folds of St. George's cross" (the flag) now flying from the Arab ship and thought how pleasing it was to see the ensign "sheltering those who were lost; helpless and hopeless slaves."[15]

According to the myth, the Royal Navy spent a great portion of the nineteenth century trying to suppress the slave traffic, and, as one essayist wrote, "many brilliant boat actions have been fought between the bluejackets and slavers." The image is one of constant struggle between brave Virtue and cowardly Vice, or, perhaps, Saint George and the dragon (the folds of Bullen's flag obviously had a double meaning for him). It was not until the nineties that Britain, in concert with Germany, made considerable headway in suppressing the trade in human flesh. It was, however, an enterprise in which she took some pride, whatever the annoyance inflicted on the entrepreneurs of other nations. The judgment of the historian Lecky in his *History of European Morals* was a common one: "The unweary, unostentatious, and inglorious crusade of England against slavery may probably be regarded as among the three or four perfectly virtuous pages comprised in the history of nations."[16]

The association of the navy with humanitarian work was comforting to the Victorian conscience. Nelson's prayer "May humanity after victory be the predominant feature in the British Fleet" represented a goal to the Englishman. He wanted to think of power as directed to greater ends than mere national glory, and a constant theme in the myth was that the navy would devote herself to the cause of humanity as a whole, regulating trade, rescuing the shipwrecked, charting unknown seas, and not simply guarding the English cause in a narrow, jingoistic way. For the English cause was conceived to be the cause of all. There was, therefore, no need to apologize for supremacy—supremacy would benefit the whole world. Truly honest men would recognize the justice in this claim and would not, therefore, attempt to compete with Britain.

To police the high seas, the navy had to act as a great patrol force, "ceaseless, ubiquitous, all-seeing." Victorian writers painted a beneficent godlike figure, protecting the weak from the strong, parceling out justice with a firm but generous hand; kind, friendly, impartial, omnipotent, one whose deeds were generally unsung. An admiral who began his career as a midshipman in 1902 quoted part of a naval prayer in a speech to the Newcomen Society: "That we may be a security for those who pass upon the seas upon their lawful occasions." He stressed both the universality of this wish and the need for lawfulness. Those nations of the earth who wished to sail might do so without fear. Provided their aims were lawful and their intents peaceful, the British navy would extend to even the smallest of them her warm cloak of protection.[17]

Thus in the national mythology the navy became not only the seagoing boy scout, helping people in distress, but also a kind of general resident referee for disputes. Some argued that the general political stability of the world in the nineteenth century (which was often referred to as the Pax Britannica) should be credited to the work of the British navy. True, there were a few armed conflicts on the European continent, but no holocaust, no world war. The reason given for this general claim was that all conflicts were localized because Britain had command of the seas. Therefore there could be no warfare between countries separated by salt water. Accordingly, the nations could indulge in revolutions and in significant events like the unification of Italy or of Germany without the convulsion spreading over the world. Further, this benevolent lordship of the sea was gratefully accepted by the rest of the world. "Never had the world such a kindly master," Mowat believed, and no nation was jealous of the British protectorate. He lamented its passing since he felt that the world was better off with one nation assuming these duties of suzerainty. Not everyone fooled himself that other nations were grateful for Britain's role, but most seemed to agree that things were more orderly when the navy played policeman. Britain was deemed to be best suited to the part.

120

Wilkinson felt that Britain deserved this responsibility because she had the most shipping and therefore had the most at stake. She should assume supervision for every part of the world's seas which was not already under the jurisdiction of a "strong and civilized power."[18]

The image of the navy as the bastion of peace is seen not only in the claims that navies (unlike armies) are peace-loving, but also in the genuine feeling that the British navy was so obviously impartial, such a thoroughly disinterested server of justice, that her very strength served the cause of peace among nations. In a chapter titled "Can Wars Be Prevented?" Admiral Eardley-Wilmot gloomily concluded that they could not, largely because the world no longer accepted the British navy as the guardian of the seas. His book was written just after the close of the Washington Naval Conference of 1921, and he regretted the missed opportunity of joining the navies of Great Britain and the United States in a giant, neo-Victorian, peace-keeping force. He deplored the whole idea of naval disarmament as a fruitless pursuit and thought that only superior force could prevent wars.

The date here is significant: the First World War had changed not only the stakes of the game but also (to some extent) the players. The admiral's longing, backward glance to a more orderly, prewar world illustrates the force as well as the decline of the Victorian navy myths.[19]

We have seen the navy symbolize the empire, the moral principles of freedom and justice, and the divinely appointed arbitration of those principles for other nations. Finally, the navy also symbolized the greatness of the country that begat it. The Englishman defined the stature of his nation by its military and moral strength. Ships of the fleet became visual symbols of this position in the world: "We turn for safety to our stately ships and dauntless sailors," Herbert Hayens stated, "with a confidence nurtured by the heroism of the ages. When they fail us, Great Britain will be numbered no more among the nations of the earth" (note that she would not only fall from the ranks of the great, she would cease to exist!). Similarly, a few years earlier, a publicist for the Navy League wrote that only if the navy were kept strong could Britain forge ahead, and thus "our race will have insured its predominance for another century."[20]

Many of these ideas we have been discussing can be seen in the conclusion to Commander Low's long epic poem on the sea: the symbolic quality of the flag, the idea of solitary superior virtue,

121

the watchword of all enslaved peoples who look towards British freedom and towards the hope it implies:

> Our flag now floats in every sea,
> And waves alone above the free,
> The British Union Jack.
>
> The slave who clambers on the deck,
> His shackles fall from off his neck,
> Once there he sets his foot.
>
> Our island-home's inviolate been,
> As palace of a British Queen,
> For some eight-hundred years.
>
> And shall be so until the day
> When Britain's empire fades away,
> And others rule the main.
>
> Oh Englishmen! This ne'er must be—
> This ancient realm, lord of the sea
> Must ever so remain![21]

The "lord of the sea" gradually sank from preeminence after the end of the First World War. The myth lasted well beyond that time, however, as we have seen, although it had lost its foundation in fact. But myth dies slowly and is sometimes best expressed by a later generation. In 1938 Hugh Kingsmill edited an interesting series of articles called *The English Genius*, in which he attempted in a number of areas to define what was characteristically and specifically English. The poet Alfred Noyes, in an essay "The Sea" in this collection, stated that because Britain's sea-myth incorporated a code of behavior, her tremendous advantage in sea power through the world could be an important war deterrent, a "signal flare in the black night." He felt that the navy was the last defense of international morality and humanitarianism, and he concluded with a quotation from his own poem, written to honor Nelson's birthday:

> There is no peace on earth, 'til truth returns!
> Guard then our own, while Europe learns anew
> That law, whose service only keeps men free
> One light at least above this island burns,
> One steadfast ocean-covenant still holds true;
> And Nelson's watchword thunders in her sea.[22]

Thus the fleet would symbolize Britain's moral mission: guardian of liberty, of peace, and of that "law" that defends freedom. It was not for nothing that Ruskin had likened the colonies to motionless navies; the metaphor worked both ways: the navy could symbolize both the essential freedom of English civilization and the link that created of the empire an organic union of a free civilization.

❀   ❀   ❀

We turn now to a parallel set of myths about the navy, myths that emphasized the active and defensive rather than the passive symbolic role for the fleet. We can see these myths of defense most clearly as they relate to and were articulated through the ideas of a single man, Henry Spenser Wilkinson (1853-1937), an indefatigable and effective propagandist for the navy. Wilkinson was a journalist, professor of military history at Oxford, and military expert. The whole of his active adult life was, as he put it, "the outcome of a single idea." At the age of twenty-one, he claims to have been surprised to find that Europe was full of great conscript armies, in contrast to Britain, who had a very small volunteer army in the fashion of the eighteenth century. Why should this be so, he wondered. He concluded, "The contrast seemed to me of great importance, and I was determined to understand it. This led me to become a student of war."[23]

In conjunction with Sir Charles Dilke, he made a study of imperial defense and visited the northwest frontiers of India. It became clear to him, as he wrote, that "the measures requisite for defense were dependent on a sound foreign policy, of which the keystone must be the maintenance of a Navy adequate to secure the command of the sea in war. I therefore wrote a series of essays pleading for a national policy, and then proposed an organisation for the reform of the Admiralty, an organisation which took the shape of the Navy League."[24]

In the summer of 1893 when there was one of those periodic renewals of public discussion of naval strength, Wilkinson was disturbed by an article in the *Times* written by Admiral Philip Colomb, then a leader in English naval thought. Colomb took the position that a "fleet in being" was adequate to the defense of the island to prevent invasion, and he supported Admiral Torrington's self-justification of withdrawal from direct encounter with the French at the battle of Beachy Head. The theory there was that a fleet lingering in the distance ("fleet in being") was more effective as a deterrent to invasion than a fleet engaging the enemy and possibly being defeated by it. In other words, no enemy would attempt invasion while there was the possibility that a defending fleet might recover its strength; any fleet was better than no fleet.

Wilkinson disagreed and in a reply outlined what he called the "Great Alternative," a term that was to become the subject and title of his next major book. The theory behind the great alternative proposed that Britain's survival would rest not upon a weak fleet, which might only prevent or postpone invasion, but upon complete command of the sea. "Great Britain is but a small island," he wrote, "and every island is at the mercy of whatever power has acquired maritime supremacy. I assert, therefore, that we cannot please ourselves whether to keep or neglect the Empire. We are compelled to choose between two extremes. England must either become a dependency of another Power holding the mastery of the sea or she must herself command the sea and lead the world." This is an interesting example of a common idea: that one must be First ("Top Nation" as the schoolboy phrase had it) or Last; there was no middle ground. The attitude was not based upon rational analysis (since of course the theory would not apply to other nations like the United States, for example) but was part of the mythic fear of annihilation. It is, I think, significant how often Victorians quoted the seventeenth-century naval hero Admiral Blake: "The purpose of the navy is to keep foreigners from fooling us." There was no possibility of what would today be called coexistence; England had either to be in command or to be a "mere dependency" of the nation in command. Wilkinson's position was called "jingoistic" by one section of the press, although he contemptuously disclaimed the adjective.[25]

His quarrel with Admiral Colomb in the columns of the *Times* was more apparent than real. They afterwards had lunch together and found they were in entire agreement. Admiral Colomb explained that he did not mean to suggest that Britain needed a weak fleet. Wilkinson was reassured (he did not really care to oppose respected naval authority). In a series of articles, "The Command of the Sea," Wilkinson asserted that the present navy was too weak for its proper function in case of war and suggested that reform would be in order—reform not only of the size and armament of the navy but, even more important, reform of the organization and administration of the service. The proposal brought support from Dilke, from Arnold-Foster, and from several other competent and influential

124

men. A letter to the *Pall Mall Gazette* signed by "Four Average Englishmen" took up his suggestion for an organization to move public opinion about the navy. One result of this support and interest was the organization of the Navy League, which I shall discuss later.

Wilkinson's ideas, although not popular until the latter part of the period of this study (from the mid-nineties on), were so characteristic of the kinds of ideals and attitudes of the whole of this period that he could conveniently stand for a certain quality of mind which I shall now examine. He used in *The Great Alternative* a phrase that sums up his attitude towards the navy: "A nation . . . must have a purpose. There must be a design to which it works, an aim with which it is identified."[26] It was the navy that simultaneously was to supply and symbolize this goal.

Certainly the purpose uppermost in the mind of the naval strategists and propagandists was the idea of naval supremacy, and the mythic importance of the goal is striking. The maintenance of supremacy was necessary, they believed, to the competent function of the navy, whose three (sometimes conflicting) duties were, first, the protection of maritime commerce; second, the protection of Britain from invasion; and third, the defense of communication with the empire. Britain possessed, therefore, a fleet to protect the Channel, a Mediterranean fleet to protect the ports and the access to the Suez Canal (the main route to India), and a cruising fleet to protect her coaling stations and colonial territories scattered from east to west.

It was a central fact that Britain was (and is) unable to feed or support herself from within. She was, therefore, dependent on a mercantile trade. Accordingly, the naval supremacists insisted that without absolute command of the seas, Britain would have been unable to feed, clothe, or supply herself; the assumption being that no other nation would be content to let Britain alone if she were at all vulnerable.

There are a great number of writers (particularly in this period of great international competition) who made alarming predictions of privation in case of an effective naval blockade. A children's book, *The Story of the Sea*, emphasized the vast issues at stake, telling its audience that Britain had a greater tonnage of merchant shipping than all the rest of Europe together, "all this staked upon the sea and our ability to command it!" Or compare Kipling's poem, "Big Steamers," written for a juvenile history:

> For the bread that you eat and the biscuits you nibble,
> The sweets that you suck and the joints that you carve,
> They are brought to you daily by all us Big Steamers
> And if anyone hinders our coming you starve!

It was not only the young who were to be frightened by the prospect. A member of Parliament pointed out that over two-thirds of Britain's population was fed on imported grain from "foreign" countries, and moreover that Britain never had more than three months' supply on hand at a time. (*Foreign* here means nonempire, an important distinction, since foreigners would be presumed to be unfriendly and colonists not.) Another writer agreed, stating that all of Britain's enemies knew that the quickest way to bring down Britain would be to starve her, in which case "the sea-girt fortress which Englishmen have been taught, almost as a matter of religion, to regard as impregnable could be turned into a death trap." The navy was not to be expected to bring food in wartime, nor even to protect the merchant ships, because it had better things to do, namely, to defeat the enemy. Therefore Britain needed a national granary system whereby adequate food supplies could be stored for up to six months at a time.[27]

The idea of national granaries found some temporary support, but there were many people opposed to it, arguing that such a system was infeasible. The stockpiling of grain would be only one step in the face of numerous needs of the nation in wartime, a time when the country would need not only grain, but raw materials and other foodstuffs as well. In wartime, furthermore, food might be put on a contraband list, so that Britain would be especially vulnerable to blockade and starvation. The underlying myth stressed that other nations could feed themselves; that no one but Britain imported food. The successful blockade of Germany during the First World War would indicate that this assumption was false.[28]

It is hard to say at this point whether all of these fears were merely alarmist or whether there was real substance behind them. What is perfectly apparent three or four generations later, however, is the mythic quality of the fear itself; the expressions of alarm at the threats to Britain's safety appeared too often in the popular press for the public not to take them seriously.

Parallel to the fear of starvation was the fear of invasion. The island security, which was so important in the psychology of the nation, was increasingly threatened and the subject of several episodes of public scares. Technology had narrowed the English Channel (with the new, faster steamers the journey was only four hours), and there was now no need to wait for favorable winds (a problem faced by Philip II and Napoleon). An invasion fleet assembled on the opposite shore was a real and dangerous possibility. A writer in *Nautical Magazine*, asking the question Is Invasion Impossible? fearfully answered in the negative. He felt that insufficient preparations were being made by officialdom: "Are we not enticing invasion by our crass stupidity?" Wilkinson had virtually the same point to make (although his style was more ponderous). He contended that the defense of an island consisted solely in naval victory: "This is the law of insularity. It constitutes the first principle of British policy, and it rests not upon political opinions but upon . . . the nature of an island." To Commander Low the threats to an island were vividly real: how frightful it would be for a foreign fleet to come up the Thames River to bombard London; how dreadful to have the English people surrendering to a foreigner, paying tribute, sacrificing their colonies, and starving to death. The picture of all these disasters was alarming but the obvious solution was the simple expedient of keeping the navy stronger than the navies of the next two or even three most powerful nations.[29]

Somehow the shield of the Royal Navy seemed broad enough to protect the English island security; the English never really believed that they could suffer the humiliation of invasion. Probably this was the reason for their essential tranquility and for the exasperation of those who tried to persuade the public of the plausibility of invasion. There was an apocryphal story about the great German military expert, Count Moltke, who was asked if he could invade England. He replied that he had several plans for getting his army into England but unfortunately none for getting it out again![30]

The Royal Navy had not only to prevent starvation and invasion, it was also supposed to protect the outposts of empire, whose dependence on the navy for communications with the mother island was a fact of paramount importance. Dilke and Wilkinson called the empire the "possession of the sea" and argued that not one of the colonies could survive if cut off from the sea: "From it they, like ourselves, derive their nourishment and their strength." This was a comment that reflected the mythic connection of the Englishman and the colonist, since Canada, for example, and probably other members of the empire would in fact survive. But it was

127

thought that if the fleet were vanquished, the empire would perish. The *Morning Post* remarked that "the first place in the Colonial world necessarily belongs to the Power that has the best Navy," and quoted Sir George Clarke, who had said that a navy able to maintain and keep open the communications of the empire was not merely the first postulate of national defense but the prime condition of security. Englishmen were not the only ones to believe this; the myth convinced the American admiral Alfred T. Mahan, who wrote in 1888 that British independence, the British Empire, and indeed, all of British greatness depended upon her maintenance of supremacy at sea.[31]

Considerable public pressure to visibly establish such supremacy resulted in the building program of 1889. The Naval Defense Act of that year started what was called the *two-power standard*, the object of which was that Britain should have a fleet equal or superior to the two next largest fleets combined, on the theory that she might have to face not one enemy, but two allied ones. At that particular period she feared an alliance of France and Russia, although the two-power standard also implied superiority over any future combinations. Some extremists argued that even this ratio would be insufficient. In 1892 H. W. Wilson urged a five-to-three superiority over France and Russia combined, but he acknowledged a major difficulty of definition that plagued all who talked about the two-power standard: What kinds of ships would be counted? Battleships only? Or total tonnage? Would you count overage ships? Admiral Sir Herbert Richmond also questioned the definition: the trouble with the slogan two-power standard was that each expert had his own interpretation of what could constitute superiority; the apparent precision of the term was misleading. Further, if Britain should not merely equal but exceed her nearest rivals, no one seemed sure what margin of superiority was necessary; some said as much as ten percent, others less.[32]

It is not surprising that Englishmen who saw themselves as the richest nation, both in amount of trade and in national wealth, should also see the rest of the world as being covetous of their naval supremacy. Wilkinson wrote that supreme command of the sea is a necessary ingredient to modern life, a prize every nation covets, "but every nation in Europe prefers that it should be held by England, rather than any other power except herself." He argued that England's command of the sea meant safety for all other nations, all of whom should have accepted such a situation gladly. Furthermore, the peculiar privilege of such a supremacy was that it carried with it the leadership of Europe in civilizing the rest of the world.[33] Such sentiments may seem particularly blind to a modern audience, but only to one who underestimates the force of myth. Consider the propositions: Englishmen are peace-loving and wish only to serve the cause of Good. The navy is defensive not offensive. If these premises are true, why should not foreigners also accept them? The major advantages in having a first-class navy equal to all competition would be the ability to maintain peace, since no power would be in a position to begin a war without some better prospect than the destruction of its own navy, the loss of its trade, and of its colonies. Thus Britain should be the arbiter of all wars, as well as the peace-keeping judge of the morality of nations.[34]

Unfortunately, self-appointed judges are rarely acceptable as authorities to the litigants. The inevitable competition with other nations varied, naturally, as did Britain's view of the relative strength of the European powers. At some periods, France seemed the major threat; at other times, particularly later in this period, it was Germany. As early as 1852 the "war-like columns" of France which were halted "within a few leagues of our shore" caused concern. These feelings reflect the geographical proximity of a not-inconsiderable continental power; it would be strange indeed if Britain did not fear French military might. But there was more to the fear than just France's strength. France had been the traditional enemy for hundreds of years; no generation raised on the glorious victories of Nelson and Wellington could think of France without some apprehension. The British had an instinctive dislike of the Frenchman's character; he seemed less reliable than the Anglo-Saxon, more shifty, more given to unwholesome and even immoral pursuits. He was also a competitor in China and Africa and therefore not wholly to be trusted.[35]

The myth of French enmity would be partially diminished by one world war and almost completely gone by a second; but until very late in this period many still saw France as the danger. In a pamphlet, *Our Next War*, published in 1896 by the Navy League, France and Russia were considered to be the two strongest naval powers after Britain. Swinburne warned his countrymen in "A Word for the Navy,"

> Smooth France, as a serpent for rancour,
> Dark Muscovy, girded with guile,
> Lay wait for thee, riding at anchor
> On waters that whisper and smile.

The Russian—the dark Muscovite, "girded with guile"—did have a fleet to beware, and he lurked perilously close to India. Englishmen assumed, with some justification, perhaps, that Russia was very anxious to snatch the Indian pearl from the British crown. Admiral Penrose Fitzgerald argued that the British navy should be strengthened to deal with a possible Russian attack, but he thought that the Russians were "bluffing" and thus were not an immediate danger. France was Britain's first enemy; Italy, a possible but doubtful foe; and Russia, not efficient enough, although if she were less childish, she would be a real threat: "Russians are a blustering, at the same time that they are a wily, race; they have a very good opinion of themselves."[36]

An example of the devices used to scare the general public was an anonymous story about a fictional battle of Port Said, supposedly to take place on 2 June 1886 with France the enemy. The French would attack near Suez, and, having diverted the English home fleet to the Mediterranean, would then send an invasion fleet that would gain sufficient control of the English Channel to defeat Britain on her own soil. The point of the story was that money that was spent on the fleet was simply money thrown away, since not enough was spent in the right places. Like the *Pearson's* story of thirty years later (see p. 48), the tale had a certain scary charm and may have had some effect on the navy estimates. Its complaint was common enough. Commander Low reminded the British public of the possible consequences of inattention to English greatness and lack of proper respect and care for the needs of the navy: "Let the tax-payer, who is in the habit of grumbling at the great and increasing expense of the Navy, picture to himself, for a moment, the condition of affairs were this country defeated at sea by a great power, or a combination of them . . . the humiliation of sinking to the position of Holland or Portugal, despised and pitied by the world." But were these two nations really despised and pitied? Maybe only by the British, to whom the "humiliation" (the diction is significant, I think) of being third-rate after achieving first status looms large in the myth of supremacy.[37]

By the nineties Britain was beginning to fear naval competition from Germany, whose kaiser had publicly announced his intention of competing directly with Britain in fleet strength. Wilkinson's book *Britain at Bay* contained a chapter devoted to the rise of Germany, where he discussed the deliberate creation of a powerful German state with both a strong navy and a strong army. Wilkinson admired German training, building, and efficiency but feared for Britain's life from a German challenge on the seas. At first, German national unification and imperial expansion had been hailed by Britain. Gladstone once spoke feelingly of his joy at welcoming another power to the godly mission of civilization. But later, after the turn of the century, and particularly after the kaiser's open friendliness for the Boers in the South African War, Britain began to have second thoughts. By 1909 editorials began to predict war with Germany. Indeed, had the kaiser possessed a competitive fleet in 1900 he might have become involved in the Boer War. A member of Parliament pointed out in 1909 that Germany's bellicosity should not surprise the British, since the German emperor had already announced that "the trident should be in his fist." If that should happen, he thought, Britain would also be in his fist.[38] While it is true that diplomacy and policy must be aware of potential and actual threats to a nation's safety, what concerns us here is not threat, but fear. For fear often indicates mythic belief which is deeply rooted in national consciousness and may have little or no relationship to "facts."

✿   ✿   ✿

Finally, it is necessary to consider the mythology of the navy actually confronted with war, when a nation will develop another set of images. One problem, never wholly solved, was the status of neutral powers in time of war. The Declaration of Paris of 1856, signed by Britain (although not by the United States), allowed an enemy to ship noncontraband material in neutral ships. Wilkinson thought that this provision would obviously work against British interests, and he was amazed that any ministry would have agreed to such a declaration. An M.P., writing fifteen years later, thought that Britain had traded an essential maritime right for an ephemeral concession from the French which was the abandonment of privateering. He argued that privateering could eventually have been eliminated by a strong Royal Navy, but it would be exceedingly difficult for Britain to regain what she had freely given away. The declaration was "a rash and unwise proceeding," as Lord Salisbury had said.[39]

The difficulty, of course, not widely recognized until well after the First World War, was that in time of war, with emotions at fever pitch, there are few actions that any nation will consider

131

unjustifiable in achieving victory. Thus, arguments over what constitutes contraband, what constitutes the rights of neutrals (or the rights of belligerents, for that matter) are rather fruitless. Immunity of all private property at sea would mean virtual deprivation of the British fleet of all offensive power, compelling it to look on quietly while the enemy imported all his wartime needs. In other words, the fleet would become "merely" defensive, not offensive. To a large extent, the arguments of the First World War, at least with respect to American participation, centered on this very question of naval rights and responsibilities.[40]

The worry about neutral rights was quite a real one. A possible wartime practice among maritime nations was the use of neutral shipping. But if Britain were to transfer her merchant marine to a neutral flag for protection, what would guarantee that after the war it would return to the British flag? Could foreigners be trusted to play fairly under such circumstances? Even if the merchant marine fared well, was there any reason to suppose that an emeny would actually respect the neutral flag? One author argued that since the time of the South African troubles, Britain's behavior to her enemies had been "so courteous and considerate" and her recognition of the so-called rights of neutrals so generous and ample that "we have almost forgotten that the majority of the nations are not used to be so tender when they plunge into war," a caution which was to prove prophetic. Clearly Wilkinson had a valid point that war was very much to Britain's disadvantage, especially if one could not expect other people to fight according to what one newspaper called "the laws of civilized warfare."[41] These worries are significant because they illustrate the force of the myth of supremacy.

No one questioned the absolute necessity for the maintenance of the Channel fleet; protection from invasion was vital. It had always been "the natural" policy of France to destroy the British navy, but it was thought even more likely now because of France's colonial designs. If France were to acquire command of the seas, she would blockade the British coast and land an army on British soil. Such a blockade would very quickly impoverish Britain, and between the blockade and the invading army Great Britain would be paralyzed. She could hope for no peace except on terms that would put an end to her empire and her existing national position. Curiously, when the idea is reversed, that is, if Britain were to crush the French fleet, the result would be very different. Wilkinson thought that Britain would be outnumbered if she tried to land an army in

France. She might attack French colonies, but without an army in France there would be no means of compelling French surrender. France could not be starved by maritime blockade because of her frontiers with other European nations. He concluded that in a war with France, England had everything to lose and very little to gain. Consequently, it was to her advantage to maintain peace, and only with superior strength would she frighten a potential enemy out of direct aggression.[42] His argument underscored the myth of the navy as an instrument of peace, and of the British as a pacific, law-abiding people with no nefarious designs on the rest of the world.

Wilkinson earlier stated his belief that a nation must be prepared to use force to accomplish its aims. If it is unwilling to use force, it might as well not bother. After all, the basis of every policy "is the power of carrying your design." Such an attitude went against the Liberal myth of the force of moral suasion (compare, for example, President Wilson's phrase, "There is such a thing as being too proud to fight"), which was beginning to die when Wilkinson was writing in 1895. Wilkinson feared war with France as a consequence of what he saw as Lord Rosebery's idiotic foreign policy—one of making extreme diplomatic claims which he was unwilling to defend militarily. Although Wilkinson did not urge going to war, he defended the use of force as not evil in itself. Its employment was neither right nor wrong but to be judged only in the context in which it was used.[43]

If, then, as he suggested, Britain had usually to be concerned to avoid hostilities, the question arose as to how war could best be avoided. To Wilkinson the answer was clear: war should be prevented by Britain's being strong; she should not give in at any point, since capitulation would weaken her vitality and economic strength, and she could not afford to be elbowed out of her important imperial posts throughout the world. Her best course was preparation for "prompt and complete victory at sea," which would then be the surest way to avert a major and all-out war.

In wartime the empire would resemble many islands scattered across the vast oceans, each needing the navy for local protection through constant shadowing of attacking fleets. "So long as you can keep up the shadowing game, and do not want to damage the enemy on land, your islanders can all live at ease, without a soldier, a rifle, or a cartridge. Moreover, if you can shadow every cruiser that the enemy possesses, your merchant ships will be as safe as your islands." But this task amounts to annexing the whole sea and might have been difficult for Britain to accomplish; ships cannot be spared to sit by guarding "islands" but must be out attacking. The important islands thus had to have local garrisons to defend them until they could be relieved from enemy siege. The most important island in this metaphor was Great Britain herself, which was basically no different from the other imperial islands. Clearly she had to have a force at home, but she could not (and here Wilkinson differed from other writers) simply have a Channel fleet that lurked watchfully while the rest of the fleet was out attacking the enemy. The best way to prevent invasion was to have the whole fleet away on the high seas fighting an offensive war.[44]

There are "natural laws" that come into operation if each of two belligerent states has a seacoast: the one with the fleet will naturally win in any conflict. It can blockade, it can move troops, it can inflict damage but suffer very little damage. You must defeat the enemy's army, but you can first paralyze him if you close his trading routes and blockade his ports. Wilkinson concluded, therefore, that a navy was a sine qua non of defense for a maritime nation. If your navy were strong enough, you had no need of an army at all. Britain should thus keep the fleet (or a part of it) near home because the enemy would necessarily be a European power (he dismissed the United States as unworthy of consideration). The place to fight an enemy was in front of his own ports, which is where you would find *his* fleet, bar a stray cruiser or two. Defeat the enemy's fleet, and you have won two-thirds of the war.[45]

Several naval officers agreed with Wilkinson's analysis and also subscribed to the myth of the peace-loving nation that subverted war by thoroughly preparing for it. In this case, as in so many others, the myth of the policy may, indeed, be factually accurate, that is, possession of great armaments *may* prevent war—I would not be prepared to attack such an idea. Admiral Penrose Fitzgerald protested that some misguided individuals in the country seemed to think that all war could be avoided by "the exercise of a skillful and righteous diplomacy." Preparation for war *may* lead to war when the state is known to be aggressive, but when adequate preparations are made by a rich and peace-loving nation (such as Britain), known to be desirous only of holding her own in the world and with no designs on her neighbor's property, who, then, could possibly mistake these preparations for aggressive designs? Her actions were simply calculated to deter some other aggressors. Fitzgerald called the peace party "sentimental."[46]

Among other solutions, Britain might have sought allies. Fighting alone might have been shortsighted, and perhaps a judicious selection of friends might have placed Britain in a good position. In 1902 Britain did make a break with her traditional splendid isolation when she signed the Anglo-Japanese Alliance, but it is significant that her approach to Europe was more cautious. On the eve of war in 1914 Lord Grey could still not quite bring himself to make a strong and open commitment to France, although doing so might have deterred Germany. The strength of the myth was still great.

❄   ❄   ❄

I shall conclude this chapter by reminding the reader of Wilkinson's belief in the need for a national purpose. This idea was not quite what twentieth-century fascism would later make it, but rather it reflected a Victorian romantic conception of the strivings of community, a conception that was reinforced by history and contemporary event. The naval historian J. K. Laughton once wrote that the study of English history showed Englishmen that it was to the navy and the navy alone that they owed their immunity from invasion, their extended commerce, and their vast colonial empire.[47] He was certainly not alone. Wilkinson agreed and concluded *Britain at Bay* with a plea for universal service and what he called a "nationalisation of war." He hoped that the navy would be both the symbol and the defensive arm of a united nation, one which could produce a leadership to personify the national spirit and accomplish these ends.

9

Reshaping a Myth

THE ADMIRALS ADJUST TO CHANGE

Now landsmen all, where e'er you may be
If you want to rise to the top of the tree
. . . .
Stick close to your desks and never go to sea
And you all may be rulers of the Queen's navy.

W. S. Gilbert, *H.M.S. Pinafore*

If blood be the price of admiralty,
Lord God, we ha' paid in full!

Kipling, "Song of the English"

THE *Pall Mall Gazette* WROTE IN 1896, "NOW, AS ALWAYS, THE measure of our strength is the potency of the national navy," pointing to the center of a great controversy that lasted from roughly 1885 through the First World War. The quarrel was over the need for change not only in men, materiel, and ships of the navy, but also in administration of the service and the country's naval policy. It is instructive in that it exhibits not only some of the myths that I have been discussing but a new belief in progress which ran counter to a traditional conservatism. To some extent, the admirals, both individually and collectively, represented the alarmist side, from which comes my subtitle, "The Admirals Adjust to Change." It is noteworthy, however, that a good many of the politicians and the general public supported the admirals, and that in some cases professional naval men did not take an extreme

136

position with regard to Britain's strength. The fact that nobody, apparently, seemed to worry very much about the size and strength of the navy before the 1880s was, I think, a function of a parallel fact that not a great deal had been written on naval topics except by antiquarians and armchair strategists, who naturally had a limited reading public.[1]

There was, of course, the occasional public alarm about the size of the navy that coincided with threatening international events. The navy had suffered serious neglect after the Napoleonic Wars, and the period from 1815 to 1855 generally marked an eclipse for naval reformers. The Crimean War in the fifties was an occasion for some concern over strategic threats from other countries, although in the Crimea Britain's long-time enemy, France, was her ally. French pretensions to a navy and to naval abilities did arouse some fear in a few breasts, but only occasionally. In the heyday of Gladstonian liberalism, the emphasis was on "retrenchment" and on saving money. The orthodox liberal would be unlikely to urge expansion of military expense—quite the opposite, in fact.

From the eighties on a dramatic change began. The previous generation had watched the shift from sail to steam and from wooden walls to ironclads. It was also an era of radical and swift technological improvement; armaments, ship design, and ship fittings were constantly modified. One effect of rapid change was fear. International rivalry demanded recognition that competition in armaments, as well as in words, was essential, but it was hard to adjust to the threat to Britain's preeminent position. The development of a psychologically reassuring myth, complete with image and phrase, takes time, and alterations in the look of things were coming too rapidly. The fear that Britain was competitively inadequate may have had little relation to the "true" situation (as happens with many fears), but what I am examining here is the effect of that emotion on the public image of defense. In this chapter I shall consider the myths of change under three general topics: (1) the ships and men, (2) the administration of the navy, as embodied in the admiralty; and (3) the organizations that contributed so much to public knowledge, providing both information and misinformation on the state of the navy.

❈   ❈   ❈

It was perhaps natural that criticism should center on ships, since the ships were the most visible aspect of the navy. As early as 1882 a member of Parliament urged the construction of a totally

137

new fleet of ironclads—cruisers, frigates, and torpedo vessels—with improved armaments and better trained men. Britain needed a far better system of planning for future needs than she had, and he drew the moral lesson by a parallel to France. In 1870 France had thought her army so superior that she had not even bothered to examine German competition; the result, the Franco-Prussian War, was familiar to everyone.[2]

Given the underlying myth of naval supremacy, journalists joined politicians in lamenting the state of the navy, and gradually admirals and other naval men began to express public concern. Professional criticism picked up noticeably in the latter part of the decade. An article by Admiral Penrose Fitzgerald in *Blackwood's* typified the concern of this period. Although it was published anonymously, as was customary, its air of expert knowledge was so clear that the average reader could not have mistaken that a naval man was writing. Fitzgerald deplored the fact that Britain traditionally improved her navy only in response to alarming "incidents"; he pleaded for a more orderly, systematic, and rational approach to reform. Fitzgerald noted that the British navy was still in first place at that time, but that France was a very close second; Italy, third; Russia, fourth; Germany, fifth; Austria, sixth; Turkey, seventh, "and the rest nowhere." He pointed out that there were, essentially, two extremes in building a navy: one could build great defensive power depending upon heavily armored ships with heavy but slow guns; or one could build light, fast ships with little armor but great offensive power. France, he assumed, had chosen the first option and Italy the second, but Britain had tried to be somewhere in the middle. Unfortunately, the vast seas for whose safety the British navy was responsible dictated that her ships had to have a great coal allowance (that is, a large portion of the cubic capacity of a ship had to be available for fuel), significantly more than French ships, which fought closer to home and therefore closer to their coaling stations. This situation not only made comparisons of design difficult, but it also meant that naval architects were greatly limited in their capacity to meet competition; there was no point to designing ships that would have to be restricted to a small area of maneuver or to a narrow function in the fleet.[3]

Sir Edward J. Reed, a naval architect and member of Parliament, in a lecture at the Royal United Service Institution in June 1888, tackled this very problem. He recommended a great expansion in the number of cruisers in the British navy since cruisers served a dual purpose as both defensive and offensive weapons. Reed was also unhappy at the mistakes that were then being made in determining the size of the vessels, their armament, their armor, and their speed. He worried that the inadequate speed of the newly built cruisers would render them obsolete very quickly. Acknowledging a little wryly that every time he had identified design mistakes for the admiralty, the admiralty very obligingly made corrections in the specifications, he wondered how long Britain could afford such an ad hoc approach to naval planning.[4]

The concern over numbers of ships is very misleading and confusing to the modern reader, since very rarely did one expert's figures tally with another's. The explanation is that tactical superiority of the British navy over any potential enemy involved not simply a matter of numbers, but also the age, speed, quality, armament, and armor of the vessels involved. The weights of these factors were constantly being juggled; thus it was virtually impossible to compare ships on a one-to-one basis. Even had it been possible to construct a perfectly adjusted comparison of the size and strength of national fleets, the varying roles assigned to the navies had to be taken into account. The British fancied that theirs was the only fleet in the world that had such a gigantic and complex task: it had not only to defend the home island and the empire; it had to attack a possible enemy, repel invasions, police the seas, and—probably most important—secure the continual flow of British commerce. An editorial in the *Times* in 1888 made the interesting prediction that in case of war an enemy's commerce would virtually disappear from the seas (the inference was that it would be transferred to neutral flags), and therefore the enemy's cruisers would have no other task than to attack Britain's shipping. Britain's cruisers, on the other hand, would have the double duty of offensive attack and defensive protection of British commerce. She would therefore need not only some numerical superiority over an enemy but *vast* superiority. Such alarmist talk, no doubt, did some good in stirring up reform and in stimulating a building program. The difficulty was that alarm became entrenched in the mythology and probably had a negative effect in making the British public so concerned with numbers as to become almost paranoid about the possible threats to its safety.[5]

The naval maneuvers of the summer of 1888 confirmed the public's concern for the navy. A naval officer argued that the summer maneuvers showed the serious weaknesses of the fleet: many of the ships listed as active in naval annuals proved too slow or underarmed or unsuitable for other reasons. Thus even the published lists could not be relied upon for accurate information about naval strength! Other experts supported this argument, pointing out that Britain was following a dangerous course in maintaining in commission so many obsolete ships which were "quite unable either to fight or to run away," a very backward-looking policy.[6]

There was also discussion and disagreement over what weaponry should be installed on the new ships. Some writers opposed the new large guns as being inefficient, expensive, and hard to repair. An editorial in the St. James Gazette argued cogently that since all machinery could break down, one needed guns which were hand-operable in an emergency; the "monster guns" were far too expensive and too dependent upon their machinery: "We put too much faith in engines; the engine has no heart." According to the Gazette it was high time to return to Nelsonian days of old, when the navy could depend on the dash and enthusiasm of the bluejacket "whose resource and recuperative force in the face of catastrophes of all sorts have been tested until they have become proverbial all over the world."[7] The paper's comment illustrated an old myth that men were greater than machines because they had heart and courage (see chapter 5). A new belief in technology, with which we are very familiar in the twentieth century, was beginning to change the myth of man-over-machine.

But while some people were sentimental about the past, others were determinedly forward looking. An article in the Pall Mall Gazette on the relative merits of broadside versus end-on arming of ships advocated the superiority of the method of stern-and-bow rather than broadside guns as particularly advantageous for pursuit vessels (the admiralty had just adopted this policy). The author dismissed as hopelessly old-fashioned the attitude embodied in an old-timer's remark: "Oh, but a British officer will lay himself along side the enemy and fight it out, broadside to broadside." It was, of course, not only old-fashioned but rather romantic in its assumption of a gentlemanly, "fair" way of fighting. Furthermore, as the Gazette pointed out, an end-on approach gave the enemy a far smaller target and meant that pursuit vessels were able to fire while pursuing.[8]

One difficulty in embracing a modern approach was that technological changes were made very much more rapidly than they ever had been in the past. The changes that occurred over the course of the queen's reign were quite startling: In 1841 the navy

140

began the slow substitution of steam for sail, a process not completed until 1862. Guns were placed on pivots, an important development that helped to defend the extremely vulnerable paddlewheel vessels. The screw engine then replaced the paddle wheel. The French armored vessels in the Crimea in 1854 impressed the British officers and encouraged the admiralty to imitate them. In 1861 a new era was begun with the launching of the *Warrior*, an iron-hulled ship. At first the use of iron plating four and one-half inches thick did not extend to the ends of the ship but protected only the central section. Later a way was found to plate the whole hull without excessive loss of buoyancy. The last quarter of the century saw the development of breech-loading guns, improved powder, better armament, use of steel rather than iron, better engines, and the substitution of machinery (steam, electric, or hydraulic) for manpower in the handling of heavy tasks like moving guns or loading cargo.[9]

These sixty-odd years of accelerated change illustrate how difficult it is for a social myth to keep pace with actual circumstance. When the myth lags seriously behind, the public becomes uneasy. Probably two of the most revolutionary and (to the public) frightening developments were the submarine and the torpedo. These were frankly offensive weapons and could not be justified by the myth of the peaceful, defensive navy. France was the first to use the submarine as an efficient weapon, and the British admiralty only slowly took it up. By 1911, however, the navy was reputed to have over seventy submarines and was beginning to develop the mystique of the submarine service. Britain was somewhat more progressive about the torpedo, but officialdom also did not sufficiently gauge its destructiveness at first. One expert suggested that large ships could easily be protected from torpedoes by the use of steel wire nets hung out on booms thirty feet from the hull, which sounds a cumbersome contrivance at best. Technological reformers also faced the need to spend public money wisely, on proven innovations. But no one could predict accurately what the next naval war would involve. Each writer had his own pet theory. Sir William Clowes visualized the next war as a struggle between battleships. He contended that it would be briefer than previous naval wars but much bloodier and more costly. A naval lieutenant, in one of the Royal Naval Handbooks, argued that speed would be the main factor and that the greatest weapon would be the torpedo. He urged greater public knowledge and support of the torpedo development. The admiralty and the government were understand-

141

ably inclined to make haste slowly, since technology might render much of the then present efforts obsolete in a few years. Their foot dragging probably reflected their suspicion of change; it certainly did very little to assuage the fears of the general public.[10]

As if there were not enough to worry about, a further problem was brought to light in the nineties. It was all very well for politicians and admirals to argue about numbers of ships and guns, but a ship was worse than useless if it lacked the men to run it. The Naval Defense Act had nearly doubled the number of ships but had made hardly any provision for increasing the men. Part of the problem was that the system for recruitment was faulty. There was a nomination system for officers only. A nomination system for engineers as well as for lieutenants would mean getting "gentlemen" as engineers. It was a curious kind of social snobbery that decreed that the bridge should be a spot for gentlemen and the engine room should not. This had been the traditional approach of the Royal Navy, but, as the *Globe* remarked, the engine room in battle was second only to the bridge; sometimes one even found gentlemen who were "gifted with just as much brains as anyone else" and who would therefore be a credit if put in charge of the machinery.[11]

Ambivalence about staffing the navy illustrates the Victorian era's uncertainty about many of its values. Would it be better to have the traditional social system continued, complete with tested ethical standards of behavior, or go along with modernity and cashier the old in favor of the new? Could one possibly have Progress without sacrificing the good old ways? There were some who thought not. The opinion of the *St. James Gazette* was conservative: a country becomes great through the quality of her men, not through her technology. Rome was not saved from the barbarians by her engines, by her catapults, or by her Greek fire (but, one may remark, neither was she saved by her men). It was a great mistake, the *Gazette* thought, to trust engines and not their masters. Spenser Wilkinson agreed, arguing that the new Dreadnought class of battleships sacrificed medium guns for speed, a fact he considered doubly unfortunate, since the crew's morale would suffer at the thought of being at a disadvantage. Dreadnoughts' speed would enable them to catch an enemy, but their inferior firepower would be a drawback when they reached him. Wilkinson thought that the spirit of the men was a far more important factor than gun-range in the winning of battles—a typical attitude in the English naval myth.[12]

❀   ❀   ❀

In the late-Victorian period the pressure for reform in the navy came to a head in the demand for change in its policy-making board—the Board of Admiralty. As it existed in the nineties, the Board of Admiralty was like a cabinet to the first lord of the admiralty, who was a civilian, a member of Parliament (thus responsible to Parliament), and a member of the cabinet. The board included a number of sea lords, who were commissioners of various departments. It controlled naval administration, defined policy, and was the organizing force behind Britain's sea power. Very broadly, it directed the maritime arm that safeguarded the kingdom from invasion, protected the food supply and British commerce, and bound the empire together—no small responsibility.

Criticizing the admiralty was not a new sport by any means. Everyone had his favorite story of admiralty incompetence. The *United Service Magazine* discovered to its astonishment in 1881 that a new "Manual of Fleet Manoeuvres" had been issued, but the admiralty had restricted officers' freedom to read and study it for fear that it might fall into the hands of the enemy![13] Many Victorian writers pointed out that even the great Nelson had had his difficulties with the admiralty, and it is perhaps axiomatic that administrators are not loved by commanders in the field. Nevertheless, criticism came to a head in the nineties, probably because so much more seemed to be at stake. While Britain had been supreme mistress of the seas, whatever system (or lack of system) she operated under seemed to suffice; "muddling through" was well established. The admiralty might have been inefficient, it might have been slow, it might have been incredibly blind; but Britain's navy was undeniably the finest, and Britain indisputably ruled the waves, so the system must have worked. When supremacy is threatened, the complaints become more urgent.

The myth of a bumbling (but somehow quaintly attractive and lovable) officialdom, whose frailties one indulgently tolerates, is caricatured in Gilbert's and Sullivan's *H.M.S. Pinafore*. The "ruler of the Queen's Navy," Sir Joseph Porter, K.C.B., takes considerable pleasure in the perquisites of his position and explains to the audience that all that is necessary to rise to the top is to be a good politician: "stick close to your desk and never go to sea." The character was popularly supposed to have been based on the career of the Right Honorable W. H. Smith, who was at the Admiralty when "Pinafore" was playing on the London stage. In 1879, when Smith received an honorary D.C.L. degree at Oxford, some rowdy

143

students sang snatches of the operetta's songs and hung a pinafore over the balcony of the theater during the ceremony.[14]

What was at issue, basically, was a question common to all democratic governments: How could there be an efficient, competent, professional military service that would be ultimately under civilian control? The conflict in earlier times had not been crucial; now it was. The older myth had held that while parliamentary control was desirable in theory, administrative efficiency was of no importance since Britain's glory was won at sea by the skill and daring of her naval commanders.

Gradually through the eighties the chorus of complaint became louder. Admiral Sir R. Spencer Robinson wrote a book in 1886 called *Admiralty Reform* in which he confronted this problem of ultimate responsibility. One grave difficulty with parliamentary control was that it inevitably made naval policy a matter of political dispute. Robinson argued (and more and more people agreed with him) that the defense of the country should not, and must not, be a matter of party. However, he conceded that if the admiralty were not subject to Parliament, its blunders might never come to the attention of the public. It was vital for the welfare of the nation that the people—through their elected representatives—be able to direct their own defense. His own particular suggestion for reform was to make members of the board individually responsible to Parliament rather than to the first lord; in other words, make the board less of a cabinet and more of a committee.[15]

But the result of individual responsibility would inevitably be the fractionation of the board, with individual members pulling against each other. Not all naval men agreed with Robinson that parliamentary control was desirable. As Admiral Penrose Fitzgerald complained, if you had a politician administering the navy, you were apt to have a politician's viewpoint, a partisan policy. In Fitzgerald's view, it was the fact of having had a civilian in sole charge that had caused all the difficulties of the preceding twenty years. The alternative, professional control of a professional service, seemed preferable to many writers; at least one would then have a more expert analysis of the needs of the navy, and one would not have, as Spenser Wilkinson once complained, civilians on the admiralty board who knew nothing about war and were unable to plan properly for the country's defense. He was very scornful of the naiveté of a common assumption that if war did break out, the cabinet could *then* send for some distinguished naval men who would tell them what to do! As Wilkinson said, there was a very "old world flavor" about this, reminiscent of the days of the Armada. Britain could ill afford such a leisurely policy.[16]

Not all writers agreed, however: the St. James Gazette praised the incumbent admiralty as on the whole the most sensible, businesslike, and patriotic board that had occupied Whitehall for more than twenty years. It applauded the naval building program and hoped that the admiralty would shake itself free from bondage of overdependence on superscientific "experts," who "treat men as if they were machines, and machines as if they were infallible." On the whole, however, there was general support for the Times, which commented impatiently on Lord Salisbury's request that the public should trust its elected officials: most politicians showed no evidence of having grasped the realities, seemed to be constantly involved in pettifogging political details, unable to see the forest for the trees, and thus unworthy of the public's trust.[17] (Both statements illustrated a popular myth of naval competence versus political incompetence.)

There were many suggestions for reform; each person had his own pet scheme. Spenser Wilkinson urged the creation of a general staff for the navy where only one man would be in charge who would be really responsible for policy and for efficiency: "Knowledge means a man, not a committee; and the knowledge wanted is of war." The only way to have knowledgeable people was to have expert people, and the only way to have expert people was to have people really responsible for their tasks. Anonymity was the curse of both services, making it far too easy for the admiralty to hide its ineptitude.[18]

Contemporary comment reflected the conflict between these two myths of civilian democratic control and professional skill. Many writers wanted an expert Board of Admiralty who had great knowledge of sea service and of sea power, but they also wanted members of this board to have a good deal of political savoir faire. The Globe urged a reconstitution of the board in order that departments should be under the effective control of the individual sea lords, who were, of course, professional naval men. Naval estimates could then be scanned carefully, department by department, by a parliamentary committee; but the navy would not have to suffer as it always had done at the hands of the treasury. The paper felt that the Board of Admiralty then ought to have the courage to resign if it felt collectively that the navy was not getting what it needed.[19]

It was primarily fear that triggered the public outcry, fear of being deceived, both by parliamentary representatives and by professional navy men. In 1897 G. W. Steevens, a journalist who specialized in military questions, attacked Mr. Goschen, the First Lord of the Admiralty, for the naval estimates he had presented to Parliament. Steevens was concerned not so much with whether the estimates were adequate as with Goschen's seeming inability to know if they were adequate or not! Was the country being asked to accept a First Lord who was so woefully ignorant of his own department that he could not even justify the expenses he was presenting? Popular articles of the period echoed this fear of being victimized by false information and of being unable to force either the government or the admiralty to provide accurate data. As one military journalist rather bitterly remarked, "The public very rarely knows the truth about anything naval." His conclusion was that the public simply had to trust the admiralty; but those who had no especial confidence in naval men wondered if this were the best solution.[20]

Whatever the merits of any particular reform scheme, the British public pressed its concerns on the government. In 1885 Tennyson had written one of his more famous poems called "The Fleet," some lines from which were frequently quoted by the critics for the next twenty or thirty years:

> You, you, if you shall fail to understand
> What England is, and what her all-in-all,
> On you will come the curse of all the land
> Should this old England fall
> Which Nelson left so great.

The British did not want a government more concerned with political power than with England's defense, a myriad of politicians unaware of the fateful consequences should England's fleet be insufficient for a challenge. Tennyson's poem threatened such politicians with disgrace and predicted that the "wild mob" would evict them if they ignored the navy. But unfortunately, it would then be "too late, too late."[21]

It is outside the scope of this book to treat in detail the response of the government to the public outcry, since my major concern here is not with naval history but with the myths of that history, and the subject of naval history is well covered in standard and special studies of the period. Modernizing the admiralty was largely the work of individual people like John Fisher and came primarily through the force of their own personalities, not from legislative change. What is interesting here is the way in which the myth of muddling through, of an incompetent but essentially harmless admiralty, was challenged by the circumstances of national competition and transformed into a myth of change. Change began to substitute belief in progress and technology for the old reliance on a stout heart and the luck of the amateur.[22]

       ✿   ✿   ✿

It remains to look more closely at some of the agencies for altering myth, since the increased influence of the public on national policy and thus on the naval myths came quite directly from increased knowledge of the problems, or, more accurately, from an assumption of greater knowledge. Several societies were founded for the purpose of extending public information about the sea and about the navy. Chronologically the first of these was the Navy Records Society, which was established in July 1893 under the primary impetus of Sir John Knox Laughton. Laughton, together with other distinguished men such as Vice Admiral Philip Colomb, J. R. Thursfield, C. H. Firth, Sidney Lee, and Sir Alfred Lyall, established the society on the model of the Early English Text Society and other historical organizations of the Victorian period. Their purpose was to render more accessible the sources of naval history and elucidate questions of naval archeology, construction, administration, organization, and social life.[23]

Laughton's idea was to do for naval history what the Shakespeare Society, the Chaucer Society, and the Camden Society had done for English literature and history. The Society agreed to publish a series of volumes, and the first volume, *State Papers Relating to the Defeat of the Spanish Armada*, edited by Laughton himself, was completed in 1894. David Hannay, Sir Clements Markham, and T. A. Brassey were asked to edit papers, and forty-two volumes had appeared by 1912. The Society had 400 members by late 1895 and 500 in 1896. The major significance of the Navy Records Society lay in bringing the serious study of naval history to the attention of nonmilitary historians, and it had much to do with making naval history a respectable branch of the parent discipline.

Another early organization that assisted in popularizing the navy and naval matters was the Royal United Service Institution. It was primarily a professional society with member officers meeting monthly to present papers on military life and technology. In its early years the matters discussed were mostly of a technical nature;

but its scope broadened, and since it was not limited to the officer class it reached high officials in the government and helped influence policy. The institution maintained a library, published a journal and generally served as a forum (for a time, really, the only major one) for public discussion of military questions. One writer called it a "powerful" influence for good.[24]

A more specifically public and popular organization was the Navy League, founded in 1895. This group had the particular purpose of alerting the public to what it considered the dangerous deficiencies in naval defense and naval building. The objects of the Navy League were:

1. To bring home to everyone in the United Kingdom the fact that raw materials and two-thirds of the food were seaborne; therefore, protection of commerce was vital
2. To inform the public that expenditure on the navy was "ordinary insurance" that no sane person would grudge
3. To enlist support for maintaining an adequate fleet
4. To insist that the navy question lay above party politics
5. To explain by lectures and the dissemination of literature throughout the empire how naval supremacy, "the heritage handed down by generations of British seamen," had been alike the source of national prosperity and the safeguard of the liberties of the people in periods of stress
6. To bind together the empire by upholding the principles of a national policy based on seapower[25]

Many prominent people, admirals, and journalists were members of the Navy League (Spenser Wilkinson, whom I have discussed before, was a conspicuous defender and indefatigable propagandizer), and the league apparently acquired a great deal of financial support in its early years. A league report published in 1897 congratulated itself on its progress in awakening the public to naval needs and vowed to continue a barrage of criticism of the government for its slowness in implementing an adequate naval program. This same report of 1897 advertised Navy League literature available for use in schools and noted that £2,453 had been spent on publication and propaganda in the previous year. A Navy League pamphlet published in 1896 claimed that the league had distributed over a hundred thousand leaflets.

Admiral Sir R. Vesey Hamilton, a firm supporter of the Navy League, wrote a series of letters to newspapers in July of 1895 informing them of the purposes of the Navy League. These letters were later published as a pamphlet and were apparently fairly successful in attracting support for the organization. In one of these, he demonstrated that the whole of Britain's history had been a product of her power on the sea; with sea power Britain had managed to acquire Canada, South Africa, Australasia: "Are you British people of Great Britain willing to continue to watch, unmoved, the steady advance of the navies of other States, in ships, in guns, in numbers of men, towards equality with ourselves and, with that advance, to witness constant growth of danger to your joint heritage and your place in the world?" Clearly the answer to this question would be no. He went on, then, to argue that "The Navy League has been created to arouse before it is too late, a perception of these facts among all men of our race who have minds broad enough to apprehend their import, and hearts subject to the impulses of British blood. To quicken the recognition that command of the seas is the deep, fundamental necessity of the whole British people."[26]

Admiral Hamilton also sent letters to colonial governors, to mayors, to boards of trade, and to various other influential people to acquaint them with the purposes of the Navy League, again emphasizing the necessity of broad imperial thinking and the importance of the destiny of the British race. A letter to the *Pall Mall Gazette* in March 1895, signed "Ignotus" and possibly written by Hamilton, lamented the old-fashioned, amateur quality of naval policy. Ignotus claimed that the public could not possibly judge the effectiveness of naval estimates from year to year and, therefore, reforms urged by the Navy League should be adopted: "Government by periodical panic is the only substitute for the Navy League; a policy of alarms and excursions instead of one of steady progress."[27]

Throughout the twenty years before the First World War, the League alternately cajoled and chivied the government and the empire for their inaction on Britain's defenses. The league thought "imperially," as the phrase had it, and the Navy League *Quarterly* of January 1913 remarked, "Nothing is so gratifying as to read of the spirit with which the dominions are taking up their part of the burden." The league was immensely popular, although its loud and boisterous actions were not to every taste; many serious-minded experts, people like Sir John Laughton, obviously thought that the league was on the lunatic fringe. Laughton wrote contemptuously of the league that "it does not strengthen its arguments by the suggestion of impossible contingencies."[28]

Nevertheless, there were some people who thought the Navy

League had not gone far enough and accordingly founded a new organization in 1908, The Imperial Maritime League. This was a brainchild of two superpatriots, Harold Fraser Wyatt and L. Graham H. Horton-Smith. These two, along with many other people, affected to discover that the Navy League after the Liberal party's electoral triumph in 1906 had become simply the stepchild of the Liberals and thus had proved inadequate to render the necessary disinterested service to the public. As Wyatt and Smith put it, the committee of the old Navy League "became the mere bond slaves of Sir John Fisher."[29]

The general aim of the new league was summed up in Wyatt and Smith's book: "Increase in the sea power of the British peoples; their closer union; and their intra-imperial organization for defense." The specific goals were:

1. Command of the sea as the national policy
2. Creation of a strategy department in the Admiralty
3. Adoption of a standard of naval strength, the old, so-called two-power standard, but with a margin of ten percent, and with the further qualification that the two-power standard should have no application to cruisers, in which a much larger British superiority was considered necessary
4. Fulfillment of the old league's duties (i.e., the Navy League), specifically, the spreading of information about the British Empire and naval supremacy
5. Increase of British seamen for British ships, it being considered extremely dangerous to have foreign officers and foreign seamen in ships of the British Mercantile Marine.

The new league announced that it would attack opposition wherever it found it, no matter what party should be at fault. It denounced the new socialists and the supporters of the present (or Liberal) government, whom it called "Little Englanders," and it asked all who would support these aims to help by joining the league in subscription.[30]

The league established naval brigades and companies in various parts of the country and had branches throughout the empire. Two of their more effective gimmicks were the establishment of essay contests and brigade companies among the young. At a meeting of one of these junior naval brigades, a captain of the Royal Navy made a speech to the assembled youths, stressing, at least by implication, the racist qualities of the Imperial Maritime League. The speech was fairly typical of most of the league's propaganda: "You English boys often do not realize the great privileges, the great heritage, you possess simply through being born in this little island. You are far better off than the German boy or the French boy or the Dutch boy. If a foreign boy goes abroad, he must, in almost every case, go into a foreign country among people who speak foreign tongues. You English boys may follow the sun around the world and yet find yourselves always among your own people and at home." As Wyatt and Smith had said in their prospectus, "The League stands for truth—not hidden, but spoken—and it stands for faith in the God-given mission of our nation and our race."[31]

Both these organizations—the Navy League and the Imperial Maritime League—effectively used new journalistic techniques and media. Popular magazines like the *Illustrated London News* and serious literary reviews, monthly and quarterly, were drafted into service to build the myth and to educate the public. They affected officialdom, too, which began to use similar methods. Starting in 1888, the summer fleet maneuvers received wide publicity, and popular journals undertook to comment on the lessons learned from the exercises. The navy also allowed journalists to view the maneuvers from on board ship. In 1899, for example, Frank Bullen, an ex-merchant marine man and popular writer of sea stories, shipped aboard the battleship H.M.S. *Mars* to witness and record the fleet exercises. His articles for the *Morning Leader*, later published as *The Way They Have in the Navy*, were a delightful and vivid account of his experience. Bullen's diction was knowledgeable without being overtechnical, and the general public must have learned much about cruisers, torpedo boats, and destroyers. The previous year Rudyard Kipling had been invited to cruise with the Channel Squadron, and his book *A Fleet in Being* served much the same function.

The great naval reviews in honor of the queen's jubilee also were well recorded by the popular press. The Navy League published a twenty-four-page, sixpenny guide to the review, complete with pictures of the ships and articles by experts such as Lord Charles Beresford and Admiral Hamilton. Beresford was so carried away with the splendor of the occasion that he suggested that to make the Naval Review a complete success and to test the fleet captains, the whole fleet should get under way and pass the royal yacht, which would be anchored at Cowes as a saluting base. He conceded that this might have been a bit dangerous: "Possibly

151

a few accidents would occur, but it would be a capital display of seamanship and the art of handling ships, and no fleet in the world could execute such an imposing maneuvre so well as our own!"[32]

After the death of Queen Victoria in 1901 a number of retrospectives of her reign appeared. The one published by the *Illustrated London News* contained an article by W. Laird Clowes, naval expert and correspondent for the *Times*, titled "Navy in the Victorian Era." Looking at the navy as it was in 1837—essentially still a Nelsonian navy—and what it had become by the turn of the century, he found the changes to be nothing short of revolutionary. In spite of Whitehall conservatism of the "blindest and most pitiful type," the navy had emerged into a modern era. The admiralty, which in 1828 felt it should discourage the use of steam, was now forward-looking and progressive.[33] The myth of the Victorian navy, nostalgically looking back to a more romantic, heroic (and simpler) era, was dying. The myths of supremacy remained, now partly undergirded with a belief in progress and change.

Part 5

CONCLUSION

10

The End of the Myth

WHY DID THE SEA-MYTH DIE? IN FACT IT IS NOT ALTOGETHER DEAD. At a cocktail party in London not long ago, a middle-aged woman inquired politely about my research. She seemed slightly skeptical about social myth and about the particular ones that I was interested in until I mentioned Nelson, to which she responded fervently: "Oh Nelson! But he was *very* glorious, wasn't he?" The same attitude might be distinguished in the four rooms of Nelsoniana in the Greenwich Museum and on the *Victory*, still moored in Portsmouth harbor and still a shrine. Sir Harold Nicolson tells a story that shows that some elements of the naval mythology had not completely gone by 1941. The naval adviser to the Ministry of Information, Lieutenant-General W. H. L. Tripp, was asked why there were no official photographs of the end of the German ship *Bismarck*. He replied, "Well you see, an Englishman would not like to take snapshots of a fine vessel sinking." Nicolson had no great opinion of the man, but he clearly thought his explanation the correct one: a sinking ship, even an enemy's, deserves to be treated with respect. Nicolson quoted Balfour: "I do not stare at a gentleman in distress."[1]

Myths do not die abruptly; they fade away like the ebb of great waves whose echoing pulses lap against the shore long after the crashing combers are gone. Although English children will probably still think the navy a more glorious career than the army, still read the nautical adventure stories of Arthur Ransome, still thrill to the tale of Drake's fireships, still remember that it was King Alfred who invented the navy and Nelson who "expected," too much has changed for these to be operant social myths any longer. The characteristic Victorian myths of the sea are virtually dead. Battleships are no longer the invulnerable monarchs of the ocean, prey as they now are to missile and air attack. If destruction, launched from land base, can rain upon any point in the globe, warfare as the nineteenth century knew it is over. No longer will the navy be expected to convoy huge fleets of men, supplies, and munitions. No longer can the navy ring Britain's shores with impregnable defenses. (It was lack of air superiority over the Channel, not Britain's fleet, which forced Hitler to abandon his invasion plans in 1940.)

The security of islandhood is also gone. Britain's destiny and safety are now apparently *with* Europe rather than apart from her. There is nothing "splendid" in isolation, now, only the danger of being left behind, economically and militarily. The economic and political nationalism of the late Victorian period will not suit an increasingly interdependent world. Even a Gaullist France recognized that peace and security depend to a large extent upon cooperation with one's neighbors.

Finally, also, the twentieth century scorns the nineteenth century's view of race and national destiny. Hitler's legacy has been a worldwide distaste for the malignant results of racism, and modern science has questioned or completely rejected many earlier conclusions about inherent capacities. If the Victorians were too conscious of their superiority to lesser folk, they at least believed that superiority imposed greater burdens of responsibility toward the less fortunate. But most peoples do not want to be looked after; they want to look after themselves, to compete on an equal footing with other nations, to have their fair share of the world's goods. The world does not want the British navy to police the seas and settle quarrels; it needs to learn to obey international law that is truly international. And national greatness is probably no longer the glittering goal it once was. Size creates difficulties; wealth brings guilt and breeds envy.

The Victorian's myths served a national and cultural image that is not viable as the twentieth century draws to a close. Other nations have inherited Britain's mantle and seem to have suffered some of her fate as well. Man needs his myths; they tell him who he is, why he exists, and how he must act. But the world changes faster than the myths can change; it remains to be seen if man can reshape his past (and thus his image of himself) in time to meet the future hurtling toward him at an alarming speed.

Bibliography

SOURCES

The Inculcation of the Myth

MYTH IS ABSORBED THROUGH A NUMBER OF EDUCATIONAL AND JOURNALISTIC sources in the society. Children may be the most susceptible to the establishment of myth, and hence those influences on their attitudes—from Nanny's nursery tales through the surreptitiously read adventure stories to the school textbooks and the admonitions of teachers and parents—all have a profound effect in building social attitudes. But the influences do not stop at adulthood. In a literate society people are subject to a constant barrage of information much of which reinforces myth. Probably the element most significant to the late-nineteenth century was the journalism of the period. Today it might be television, or perhaps popular music; in the 1930s and 1940s radio became important. Two factors affected the press in the last two decades of nineteenth-century England: the increase in the size of the reading public (partly a result of increased leisure for reading, particularly among the middle and lower classes), and the development of a more modern style of journalism that was aimed at a mass audience and used modern techniques of journalism such as sensationalism, brighter layout, and promotional schemes to build circulation. New techniques of reporting also meant that newspapers were a much more important source of information than they had been previously. With virtually no other news media available, the newspapers' potential for influence was much larger than it is today. An increased reading public meant a better-informed public and therefore a public more influential in national affairs.

The nineteenth-century periodical press was also important to the reading public. There were a great number of reviews dating from early in the century, and others sprang up after the mid-century when paper duties were repealed. There were, basically, two types of periodicals: the review which was chiefly literary, offering critical comment on newly published work, and the general periodical (often also called a review), which featured articles on political and social current affairs as well as on literary subjects. Early in the century there was a close connection between the reviews and the book-selling and publishing business. Publishers frequently controlled literary criticism. Gradually, as the periodicals became more general in nature, they also became more politically and economically independent. Even at the end of the century, the reviews that remained "literary" in object contained a good deal of social criticism disguised in the form of book reviews. For example, the *Edinburgh Review*, founded in 1802, would often review political books in long articles (a group of biographies of Nelson was the subject of such an article by the naval writer J. K. Laughton).

Pamphlet literature was also greater in proportion to the population than it is today. Much of this frankly biased material was published by the various societies—the Navy League, the Imperial Maritime League, and the United Service Institution, among others—which lobbied for increased public support for the navy. The literary quality of what was merely transitory propaganda was fairly high. Many good journalists and professional navy men wrote for them (for example, Commander Charles Rathbone Low, Commander Charles N. Robinson, Admiral Philip Colomb, Sir William Laird Clowes, John Knox Laughton, Spenser Wilkinson, and many others). These men were influential in the changing of attitudes toward the navy and English history. They had acquired real expertise in naval affairs and no doubt helped to balance the flood of self-styled experts, the alarmists and antialarmists who took to print to publicize their views.

When we turn from journalism to literature we also find semiconscious myth-making, although it should be understood that propaganda that aims to change public policy may unconsciously draw on myth but doesn't necessarily deliberately change it. The laws of aesthetics notwithstanding, literature is as often instructive as it is entertaining, and it is a mistake to think that literature is more exclusively descriptive than pre- or proscriptive, even in the twentieth century.

Probably the earliest of the sea novelists who were widely read was Frederick Marryat, known as Captain Marryat. He was a sailor of great and long experience who turned novelist after his retirement from the sea. He died in 1836, but his novels were published in many editions through the century. Although he wrote of the pre-Trafalgar period (the years of the press-gang, before the ironclad and the steamship) his works set the foundation for much of the spirit that ran through the myth in the late-Victorian period; the traditions of individualism, high-minded courage, and devotion to duty were taken up by other writers. One very popular writer of a later period was another ex-navy man: W. Clark Russell (1844–1911). Russell had spent many years in the mercantile marine, and in much of his work the ulterior motive was to persuade the public of the need for reform of the merchant sailor's life.

Any consideration of literature as myth-maker must also include poetry, a form that was a good deal more popular in the nineteenth century than it is today, where it seems to have gone into eclipse. The general public's appetite for all poetry, good and bad, was large. Much of it was mediocre in style and form, but it filled an important role in inculcating the myth and contributed heavily to the romantic view of the sea. Collections of verse were common in the late-Victorian period, and collections on the topic of the sea were numerous. One, in particular, called *Sea-Music, An Anthology of Poems and Passages Descriptive of the Sea*, was edited by Mrs. William Sharp and published in London around 1888. In her preface Mrs. Sharp writes that to Englishmen the sea had always been "a dread [and] a wonder; but—so far as we know—no peoples have loved it as in these latter days it is loved by us" (p. ix). She also thought that among all northern races those with Celtic blood in their veins had been the ones who most feared, loved, and worshipped the seas. (Other writers have been more prone to consider the sea a Saxon perquisite! The labels were apparently flexible).

Quite a number of Victorian writers complained that the earlier eighteenth-century verse had been not only poor verse but also derogatory of the very subject (the sea and the English seamen) it purported to extol. Several anthologists remarked on the lack of good sea poetry in English literature (a rather surprising comment to a twentieth-century reader, perhaps, who can immediately call to mind Campbell, Thomson, Coleridge and others). Yet there was probably more sea-poetry written in the Victorian period than at any other time, and this was a significant factor in the myth-making and myth-reflecting.

Along with the poetry, those verses that are set to music become even more the creators of myth. There are a number of good sea songs in the English tradition, both landsmen's songs and chanties, or work songs, sung by landlubber and seaman alike. Many of the ballads celebrated famous naval victories: Admiral Benbow's, for example, which is still well known today. Benbow's fight against the French in 1702 against heavy odds has a number of the archetypes of the English myth: the overwhelming enemy force, the desertion and betrayal of subordinates, his bravery under fire, and his eventual death on the deck while he was still supervising the battle. Nelson's exploits also are memorialized in both signed and anonymous ballads, and there are many ballads of the Armada and other battles of English naval history.

The sea and the navy also provided material for drama and melodrama. The enforced long absence of the sailor could be a useful plot device, and the stereotypic characters of both the honest tar and the naval officer contributed to the playwright's purposes. Jerrold's *Black-Ey'd Susan* (1829) featured the simple patriotic sailor who assaults his superior officer for accosting his girl. He is tried and doomed to execution only to be saved at the last moment by the revelation of a previous heroic act, and he is released to the combined cheers of crew and audience. Lord Lytton's *Lady of Lyons* (1838) used military life as a redemptive device for the lower-class hero who not only expiates his earlier crime but also rises sufficiently in social station to get the girl of his choice. In this particular play, it is the army that provides him with the path to glory, but it could

159

as well be the navy. Such a situation also reflects the myth of the military life as a means of social mobility. Later in the century, W. S. Gilbert was to satirize this very quality of his dramas, particularly *H.M.S. Pinafore*, where "love levels all ranks," and the daughter of a captain can aspire to marry the first lord of the admiralty. Gilbert's comedy was gentle and his situations absurd, but they reflected the Victorian myths at the same time that they made fun of them.

Finally, there was juvenile literature, from popular biographies of naval heroes; histories of naval battles like the Armada and Trafalgar; accounts of life at sea; interesting discussions of naval technology, equipment, and navigation; to stirring stories of romance and discovery, fictional and nonfictional. James Macaulay, a physician turned writer, wrote a number of works for children, one of which rejoiced in the formidable title *All True: Records of Peril and Adventure by Sea and Land—Remarkable Escapes and Deliverances—Missionary Enterprises—Wonders of Nature and Providence—Incidents of Christian History and Biography; A Book of Sunday Reading for the Young.* Such an ambitious undertaking, the author hoped, would form "virtuous and Christian character in the youthful mind," and it typified the attempt to capture the young's interest and turn the twig under the guise of romantic tales of nobility and glory. Dr. Macaulay's *Thrilling Tales of Enterprise and Peril, Adventure and Heroism* was published in 1886 and *Wonderful Stories of Daring, Enterprise, and Adventure* in 1887. In his preface to the latter book he stated that he found no work more congenial than "providing suitable reading for the young," and he felt that truth was better than fiction for inspiring good and noble feelings.

In Macaulay's book *Wonderful Stories*, there are quotations from and advertisements of his other works on the endpapers. A comment typical of these advertisements quoted from what was apparently a religious periodical ran, "Fire and fight, courage and danger, enough for a whole generation of boys. Well done, Dr. Macaulay; you are second to none in telling a tale and warming the hearts of your youthful audience as you do it. Your talk is manly, and your book is a good six shillings' worth of thrilling history." It is unclear whether the boys themselves felt this way, but the parents who bought the books certainly did.

Children were just as much subject to myth-making in their school studies as in their leisure reading. One history, called *Britain on and Beyond the Sea, A Handbook to the Navy League Map of the World* (Edinburgh [1900]), was written by an assistant master at Tonbridge, a private school for boys, as a brief historical essay commenting on the map. Published by the Navy League, the handbook was dedicated to the British schoolboy, while the map was dedicated to "children of the British Empire." The map is a Mercator projection, about 10″ x 13″. All the British possessions, including the dominions, are in vivid dark red. The other countries are in paler colors: light lavender for Russia, green for the United States, and grey for China. It is officially titled "The Navy League Map illustrating British Naval History" and includes charts at the sides giving data on wealth and social condition of the empire, imports, distances, expenditures on fleets, sources of food supply, and a comparison of fleets of the principal maritime powers. At the top is a list of the major events in the naval history of the British Empire.

With such reading at his disposal no wonder the English child grew up believing that the sea was in his blood (even if he was a poor, town-bred child who never saw a large body of salt water) and believing in the destinies of his race and country. Even when he became adult there would be little in his reading to contradict these myths or replace them with others.

BOOKS

The distinction between primary and secondary source material is often a tenuous one. How, for example, does one classify an essay written thirty years after our period by an admiral who was reared and educated under the influence of the myths of late-Victorian times? Generally, I have included in the category below those works dealing with myth as subject; with the navy, historically; or with other source material in a critical fashion.

General Works (Secondary)

Auden, W. H. *The Enchaféd Flood Or the Romantic Iconography of the Sea.* New York: Random House, 1950.

Benwell, Gwen, and Waugh, Arthur. *Sea Enchantress: The Tale of the Mermaid and Her Kin.* New York: Citadel, 1965.

Berckman, Evelyn. *The Hidden Navy.* London: Hamish Hamilton, 1973.

Bonnett, Stanley. *The Price of Admiralty: An Indictment of the Royal Navy, 1805-1966.* London: Hale, 1968.

Brooks, Cleanth. *The Well-Wrought Urn: Studies in the Structure of Poetry.* New York: Harcourt, Brace, 1947.

Buckley, Jerome Hamilton. *The Victorian Temper: A Study in Literary Culture.* New York: Vintage, 1951.

Bush, Douglas. *Mythology and the Romantic Tradition in English Poetry.* Cambridge: Harvard Univ. Press, 1969.

Cassirer, Ernst. *Language and Myth.* New York: Dover, 1946.

Chase, Richard. *Quest for Myth.* Baton Rouge, La.: Louisiana State Univ. Press, 1949.

Downer, Alan S. *The British Drama: A Handbook and Brief Chronicle.* New York: Appleton-Century-Crofts, 1950.

Eliade, Mircea. *Patterns in Comparative Religion*. New York: Sheed and Ward, 1958.

Frazer, James G. *The Golden Bough*. New York: Macmillan, 1900.

Frye, Northrup. *A Study of English Romanticism*. New York: Random House, 1968.

Gardiner, Leslie. *The British Admiralty*. London: Blackwood, 1968.

Graham, Gerald S. *The Politics of Naval Supremacy: Studies in British Maritime Ascendancy*. Cambridge: Cambridge Univ. Press, 1965.

Graham, Walter. *English Literary Periodicals*. New York: Nelson, 1930.

Graves, Robert. *The Greek Myths*. 2 vols. Baltimore: Penguin, 1955.

Harrison, Jane. *Prolegomena to the Study of Greek Religion*. New York: Meridian, 1960.

Hole, Christina. *English Folk-Heroes*. London: Batsford, 1948.

Houghton, Walter. *The Victorian Frame of Mind*. New Haven, Conn.: Yale Univ. Press, 1963.

Jung, C. G. *Collected Works*. 17 vols. New York: Pantheon, 1953.

Kemp, Peter. *The British Sailor: A Social History of the Lower Deck*. London: Dent, 1970.

Laffin, John. *Jack Tar: The Story of the British Sailor*. London: Cassell, 1969.

Langer, Susanne L. *Philosophy in a New Key*. New York: New American Library, 1942.

Lewis, Michael. *British Ships and British Seamen*. London: Longmans, Green, 1940.

———. *England's Sea-Officers: The Story of the Naval Profession*. London: Allen & Unwin, 1948.

———. *The History of the British Navy*. Fair Lawn, N.J.: Essential, 1959.

———. *The Navy of Britain: A Historical Portrait*. London: Allen & Unwin, 1948.

———. *The Navy in Transition, 1814–1864: A Social History*. London: Hodder & Stoughton, 1965.

Lloyd, Christopher. *Captain Marryat and the Old Navy*. London: Longmans, Green, 1939.

———. *The Nation and the Navy: A History of Naval Life and Policy*. London: Cresset, 1954.

———. *A Short History of the Royal Navy, 1805–1918*. 3d ed. London: Methuen, 1946.

Malinowski, Bronislaw. *Magic, Science, and Religion, and Other Essays*. Glencoe, Ill.: Free Press, 1948.

Marder, Arthur J. *The Anatomy of British Sea Power: A History of British Naval Policy in the Pre-Dreadnought Era, 1880–1905*. New York: Knopf, 1940.

————. *From the Dreadnought to Scapa Flow: The Royal Navy in the Fisher Era, 1904–1919.* 5 vols., London: Oxford, 1961–69.

————, ed. *Fear God and Dread Nought: The Correspondence of Admiral of the Fleet Lord Fisher of Kilverstone.* 3 vols. Cambridge, Mass.: Harvard, 1952–59.

Mowat, R. B. *The Victorian Age: The Age of Comfort and Culture.* London: Harrap, 1939.

Murray, Henry A., ed. *Myth and Mythmaking.* Boston: Beacon, 1962.

Nicoll, Allardyce. *British Drama: An Historical Survey from the Beginnings to the Present Time.* 4th ed., rev. New York: Barnes and Noble, 1946.

Ogden, C. K. and Richards, I. A. *The Meaning of Meaning.* 10th ed. New York: Harcourt, Brace, 1952.

Parkinson, C. Northcote. *Portsmouth Point: The Navy in Fiction, 1793–1815.* London: Hodder & Stoughton, 1948.

Potter, E. B., ed. *Sea Power: A Naval History.* Englewood Cliffs, N.J.: Prentice-Hall, 1960.

Richards, I. A. *Science and Poetry.* 2d ed. London: Kegan, Paul, Trench, Trubner, 1935.

Schofield, B. B. *British Sea Power: Naval Policy in the Twentieth Century.* London: Batsford, 1967.

Schurman, D. M. *The Education of a Navy: The Development of British Naval Strategic Thought, 1867–1914.* Chicago, Ill.: Univ. of Chicago Press, 1965.

Tylor, E. B. *Primitive Culture.* 2 vols. 3d ed. New York: Holt, 1889.

Urban, Wilbur Marshall. *Language and Reality.* New York: Macmillan, 1939.

Vickery, John B., ed. *Myth and Literature: Contemporary Theory and Practice.* Lincoln, Neb.: Univ. of Nebraska Press, 1966.

Watson, Harold Francis. *The Sailor in English Fiction and Drama, 1550–1800.* New York: Columbia Univ. Press, 1931.

Weisinger, Herbert. *The Agony and the Triumph: Papers on the Use and Abuse of Myth.* East Lansing, Mich.: Michigan State Univ. Press, 1964.

Wesselhoeft, Edward C. *The Sea and the Sailor in Fiction.* Philadelphia: Published by the University, 1916.

Whiteside, Thomas. *The Tunnel under the Channel.* New York: Simon & Schuster, 1962.

Williamson, James A. *The English Channel: A History.* London: Collins, 1959.

————. *The Ocean in English History.* Oxford: Oxford University Press, 1941.

General Works

Adams, W. H. Davenport. *England on the Sea: Or the Story of the British Navy, Its Decisive Battles and Great Commanders.* 2 vols. London: White, 1885.

———. *Famous Ships of the British Navy: Stories of Enterprise and Daring of British Seamen.* London: Virtue, 1868.

Admiralty Administration: Its Faults and Defaults. 2d ed. London: Longmans, Green, 1861.

Bassett, Fletcher S. *Legends and Superstitions of the Sea and of Sailors.* London: Sampson Low, 1885.

Belloc, Hilaire. *On Sailing the Sea.* London: Hart-Davis, 1951.

Bourne, H. R. Fox. *English Seamen under the Tudors.* 2 vols. London: Bentley, 1868.

Bowles, Thomas Gibson. *Sea Law and Sea Power as They Would Be Affected by Recent Proposals, with Reasons against Those Proposals.* London: Murray, 1910.

Brassey, Sir Thomas. *The British Navy: Its Strength, Resources, and Administration.* 2 vols. London: Longmans, 1882.

Bullen, Frank T. *Our Heritage of the Sea.* London: Smith, Elder, 1906.

———. *The Way They Have in the Navy.* London: Smith, Elder, 1899.

Cababé, Michael. *The Freedom of the Seas: The History of the German Trap.* London: Murray, 1918.

Clowes, W. Laird. *All about the Royal Navy.* London: Cassell, 1891.

Dilke, Charles Wentworth, and Wilkinson, Spenser. *Imperial Defence.* London: Macmillan, 1892.

Dixon, W. MacNeile. *The British Navy at War.* Boston: Houghton, Mifflin, 1917.

Drage, Geoffrey. *Sea Power.* London: Murray, 1931.

Escott, E. H. S. *Masters of English Journalism: A Study of Personal Forces.* London: Unwin, 1911.

Ford, Ford Madox. *England and the English: An Interpretation.* New York: McClure, Phillips, 1907.

Fox, Frank. *Ramparts of Empire: A View of the Navy from an Imperial Standpoint.* London: Black, 1910.

Freeman, Edward A. *Four Oxford Lectures, 1887.* London and New York: Macmillan, 1888.

———. *Greater Greece and Greater Britain.* London: Macmillan, 1886.

Froude, James Anthony. *English Seamen in the Sixteenth Century.* London: Longmans, Green, 1919.

———. *Oceana: Or, England and Her Colonies.* New York: Scribner, 1888.

Giberne, Agnes. *The Romance of the Mighty Deep: A Popular Account* of the Ocean; the Laws by Which It Is Ruled, Its Wonderful Powers, and Strange Inhabitants. London: Pearson, 1905.

Hall, W. Clarke, and Salaman, Clement. Britain's Glory: A Popular Account of the Royal Navy. London: Swan, Sonnenschein [1896].

Hannay, David. A Short History of the Royal Navy, 1217–1815. 2 vols. London: Methuen, 1909.

James, W. M. The Influence of Sea Power on the History of the British People. Cambridge: At the Univ. Press, 1948.

Jane, Fred T. Heresies of Sea Power. London: Longmans, Green, 1906.

———. The Imperial Russian Navy: Its Past, Present, and Future. Rev. ed. London: Thacker, 1904.

Kingsley, Charles. Health and Education. New York: Appleton, 1897.

———. Plays and Puritans, and Other Historical Essays. London: Macmillan, 1890.

Kipling, Rudyard. A Fleet in Being: Notes of Two Trips with the Channel Squadron. London: Macmillan, 1898.

———. Sea Warfare. New York: Doubleday, Page, 1917.

Laughton, J. K. The Study of Naval History. London: R.U.S.I., 1896.

Leyland, John. The Achievement of the British Navy in the World War. London: Hodder & Stoughton, 1917.

Lihou, John. Suggestions for the Establishment of a Royal Naval Nursery for Sailors to Man Her Majesty's Fleet. London: James Ridgway, 1838.

Low, Charles R. The Great Battles of the British Navy. London: Routledge [1872].

Macaulay, Thomas Babington. Critical, Historical, and Miscellaneous Essays and Poems. 3 vols. Chicago: Bedford, Clarke, 1888.

Mahan, A. T. Types of Naval Officers, Drawn from the History of the British Navy. London: Sampson, Low, Marston, 1902.

Mason, Frank H. The Book of British Ships. London: Frowde, Hodder & Stoughton, 1910.

McHardy, C. McL. The British Empire: Suggested Basis for the Apportionment of the Expense and Control of the Sea and Land Forces, and the Representation of the Self-Governing Colonies in an Imperial Council, Parliament, or Congress. London: King, 1902.

———. British Seamen, Boy Seamen, and Light Dues. London: Navy League, 1899.

The Mercantile Marine in War Time. London: Spottiswood, 1902.

Middlemore, John T. The Navy in the House of Commons. London: Longmans, Green, 1909.

Moore, Admiral Sir Henry. The British and American Navies: Their Common Heritage and Traditions. New York: Necomen, 1948.

A Naval Peer [pseud.]. *Our Naval Position and Policy*. London: Longman, 1859.

Naval Reform and the Naval List as It Should Be. London: Stanford, 1861.

Navy League. *Minutes of the Navy League Meeting*. London: Navy League, 1898.

————. *Minutes of the Proceedings at the Navy League Conference to Consider the Position of This Country If Involved In War*. London: Navy League, 1889.

An Officer of the Royal Navy [pseud.]. *Popularity of the Royal Naval Service*. London: Simpkin and Marshall, 1826.

Osborn, Sherard. *On the Impressment of British Seamen and the Necessity for a Naval Militia Bill*. London: Blackwood, 1874.

Plunkett, E. *The Past and Future of the British Navy*. London: Longman, 1846.

Reed, E. J. *On the Modifications Which the Ships of the Royal Navy Have Undergone during the Present Century in Respect to Dimensions, Form, Means of Propulsion, and Power of Attack and Defence*. London: Robertson, Brooman [1859].

Richmond, Admiral Sir Herbert. *Statesmen and Sea Power*. Oxford: Clarendon, 1946.

Robinson, Charles N. *The British Fleet: The Growth, Achievements and Duties of the Navy of the Empire*. London: Bell, 1894.

————. *The British Tar in Fact and Fiction*. London: Harper, 1911.

————, and Leyland, John. *For the Honour of the Flag: A Story of Our Sea-Fights with the Dutch*. London: Seeley, 1895.

Rosebery, Lord. *Miscellanies, Literary and Historical*. 2 vols. London: Hodder & Stoughton, 1921.

Ruskin, John. *Collected Works*. 30 vols. London and New York: Chesterfield, n.d.

Shee, George F. *The Briton's First Duty: The Case for Conscription*. London: Grant Richards, 1901.

Statham, E. P. *Privateers and Privateering*. London: Hutchinson, 1910.

————. *The Story of the "Britannia," The Training-ship for Naval Cadets*. London: Cassell, 1904.

Steevens, G. W. *Naval Policy, with Some Account of the Warships of the Principal Powers*. London: Methuen, 1896.

Watt, Henry F. *The State of the Navy*. London: Chapman & Hall, 1874.

Westcott, Allan, ed. *Mahan on Naval Warfare: Selections from the Writings of Rear Admiral Alfred T. Mahan*. Boston: Little, Brown, 1944.

Wilkinson, Spenser. *Britain at Bay*. London: Constable, 1909.

————. *British Aspects of War and Peace*. London: Duckworth, 1920.

————. *The Command of the Sea*. London: Constable, 1894.

———. *First Lessons in War*. London: Methuen, 1914.

———. *The Great Alternative: A Plea for a National Policy*. London: Swan Sonnenschein, 1894.

———. *The Nation's Awakening: Essays towards a British Policy*. London: Constable, 1896.

———. *The Nation's Servants*. London: Constable, 1916.

———. *The Volunteers and the National Defence*. London: Constable, 1896.

———. *War and Policy*. London: Constable, 1900.

———, ed. *The Nation's Need: Chapters on Education*. London: Constable [1903].

Wilson, C. Holmes. *Offence, Not Defence: Or, Armies and Fleets*. London: Allen, 1907.

Wyatt, C. H. *The English Citizen: His Life and Duty*. London: Macmillan, 1894.

Wyatt, H. F. *The Enemies of the People*. London: Sampson, Low, 1911.

———. *God's Test by War*. London: Burleigh, 1912.

——— and Horton-Smith. *L.G.H.: The Passing of the Great Fleet*. London: Sampson, Low, 1909.

Popular Compilations and Picture Books

Some of the works in the previous category might legitimately be called popular in that they were written for general, not professional, consumption. The following, however, are more general miscellanies, mostly illustrated works to generate public enthusiasm for the navy.

Leslie, Robert C. *Old Sea Wings, Ways, and Words: In the Days of Oak and Hemp*. London: Chapman & Hall, 1890.

Low, Charles Rathbone. *Her Majesty's Navy: Including Its Deeds and Battles*. 3 vols. London: Virtue [1890].

Navy League. *Guide to the Naval Review*. London: Navy League, 1897.

Q, ed. *The Story of the Sea*. 2 vols. London: Cassell, 1895–96.

Robinson, Charles N., ed. *Britannia's Bulwarks*. London: Newnes, 1901.

———. *Sea Service*. London: Tuck [1893].

Russell, W. Clark et al. *The British Seas: Picturesque Notes*. London: Seeley, 1892.

———. *Sailors' Language: A Collection of Sea-Terms and Their Definitions*. London: Sampson Low, 1883.

———. *The Ship: Her Story*. London: Chatto & Windus, 1899.

Scott, Sybil, ed. *A Book of the Sea*. Oxford: Clarendon, 1919.

Shaw, Frank H., and Robinson, Ernest H., eds. *The Sea and Its Story: From Viking Ship to Submarine*. London: Cassell, 1910.

Whymper, [Frederick]. *The Sea: Its Stirring Story of Adventure, Peril, and Heroism*. 4 vols. London: Cassell [1882–85].

Technical works

Board of Admiralty. *The Entry and Training of Naval Cadets.* London: H.M.S.O., 1914.

——. *Manual of Seamanship.* 2 vols. London: H.M.S.O., 1908.

——. *A Seaman's Pocketbook.* London: H.M.S.O., 1943.

Armstrong, G. E. *Torpedoes and Torpedo-Vessels.* 2d ed. London: Bell, 1901.

Bedford, F. G. D. *The Sailor's Handbook, Containing Information in a Concise Form Which the Sailor Will Find Useful in All Parts of the World.* 3d ed. Portsmouth: Griffin, 1906.

Hamilton, R. Vesey. *Naval Administration: The Constitution, Character and Functions of the Board of Admiralty and of the Civil Departments it Directs.* London: Bell, 1896.

King, J. W. *The War-Ships and Navies of the World.* Boston: Williams, 1880.

Oldknow, Reginald C. *The Mechanism of Men-of-War.* London: Bell, 1896.

Todd, John, and Whall, W. B. *Practical Seamanship for Use in the Merchant Service.* 3d ed. London: Philip, 1898.

Histories

Included in this section are those histories of Britain and of classical Greece which directly reflected the sea myth, as I discussed in chapter 3. Childrens' texts are also included here.

Allcroft, A. H. *The Making of Athens: A History of Greece, 495–431 B.C.* London: Clive [1896].

Bury, J. B. *The Idea of Progress.* New York: Dover, 1955.

——. *History of Greece for Beginners.* London: Macmillan, 1903.

Callcott, Maria. *Little Arthur's History of England.* London: Murray, 1937 (First published 1835).

Collier, William Francis. *History of the British Empire.* London: Nelson, 1907.

Craig-Knox, Isa. *The Little Folks' History of England.* London: Cassell [1899].

Dawe, C. S. *King Edward's Realm: The Story of the Making of the Empire.* London: Educ. Supply Assn., 1902.

Dickens, Charles. *A Child's History of England.* London: Chapman & Hall, 1893.

Fletcher, C. R. L., and Kipling, Rudyard. *A School History of England.* Oxford: Clarendon, 1911.

Freeman, Edward A. *Historical Essays.* London: Macmillan, 1871.

Gibson, John. *History Made Easy: An Epitome of English History Prepared Especially for the Public Examinations.* London: Reeves & Turner, 1882.

Hayens, Herbert. *The Story of Europe.* London: Collins [1907].

Hudson, Robert. *The Romance of Our Colonies: Or, Planting the Flag Beyond the Seas.* London: Pitman [1912].

Jeffery, Walter. *A Century of Our Sea Story.* London: Murray, 1900.

Keatinge, M. W. *Studies in the Teaching of History.* London: Black, 1910.

Kennedy, Howard Angus, ed. *The Story of the Empire.* 13 vols. London: Marshall, 1897–1903.

Marshall, H. E. *Our Island Story: A History of Britain for Boys and Girls.* London: Nelson, n.d.

Mason, W. F. *A Synopsis of Grecian History, 382–338 B.C.* Cambridge: Univ. Correspondence College [1888].

Moffat's Outlines of English History. London: Moffat, Paige [1886].

Norton, Caroline Ada. *History of Greece for Children.* London: Sonnenschein [1882].

Oman, C. W. C. *An Elementary History of Greece: From the Earliest Times to the Death of Alexander the Great.* London: Rivingtons, 1903.

Robinson, W. S. *Illustrated History of England for the Middle Forms of Schools and for Students Working for the Oxford and Cambridge Local and Similar Examinations.* London: Rivingtons, 1907.

Seeley, John R. *The Expansion of England: Two Courses of Lectures.* Boston: Roberts, 1883.

Sellar, W. C., and Yeatman, R. J. *1066 and All That: A Memorable History of England.* New York: Dutton, 1934.

The Story of Greater Britain. London & Glasgow: Collins [1909].

Walpole, Arthur S. *Little Arthur's History of Greece.* London: Murray, 1901.

Biographies and Memoirs

Adams, W. H. Davenport. *Eminent Sailors: A Series of Biographies of Great Naval Commanders, Including an Historical Sketch of the British Navy from Drake to Collingwood.* London: Routledge, 1882.

Bullen, Frank T. *Recollections: The Reminiscences of the Busy Life of One Who Has Played the Varied Parts of Sailor, Author, and Lecturer.* London: Seeley, 1915.

Coate, H. E. Acraman. *Realities of Sea Life: Describing the Duties, Prospects, and Pleasures of a Young Sailor in the Mercantile Marine.* London: Gill, 1898.

Conrad, Joseph. *The Mirror of the Sea.* New York: Doubleday, Doran, 1928.

Corbett, Julian. *Sir Francis Drake.* London: Macmillan, 1928.

Eardley-Wilmot, Sydney M. *An Admiral's Memories: Sixty-five Years Afloat and Ashore*. London: Sampson Low, Marston [1926].

Haggard, H. Rider. *The Days of My Life*. 2 vols. London: Longmans Green, 1926.

Jeaffreson, John Cordy. *The Queen of Naples and Lord Nelson*. 2 vols. London: Hurst and Blackett, 1889.

Jean-Aubry, Gerard. *The Sea Dreamer: A Definitive Biography of Joseph Conrad*. Translated by Helen Sebba. New York: Doubleday, 1957.

Laughton, John Knox. *Nelson*. London: Macmillan, 1895.

———. *Nelson and His Companions in Arms*. London: Allen, 1905.

———. *Studies in Naval History: Biographies*. London: Longmans, Green, 1887.

———, ed. *From Howard to Nelson: Twelve Sailors*. London: Lawrence and Bullen, 1899.

Nicolas, Nicholas Harris, ed. *The Dispatches and Letters of Vice Admiral Lord Viscount Nelson*. 7 vols. London: Colburn, 1844–46.

Reminiscences of a British Naval Officer. Toronto: Bain, 1885.

Russell, W. Clark. *Horatio Nelson and the Naval Supremacy of England*. new ed. London: Putnam, 1923.

———. *Pictures from the Life of Nelson*. London: Bowden, 1897.

———, ed. *Nelson's Words and Deeds: A Selection from the Dispatches and Correspondence of Horatio Nelson*. London: Sampson Low, 1890.

Southey, Robert. *The Life of Nelson*. 2 vols. New York: American Book, 1895.

Warner, Oliver. *Lord Nelson: A Guide to Reading with a Note on Contemporary Portraits*. London: Caravel, 1955.

Whyte, Frederic. *The Life of W. T. Stead*. 2 vols. London: Cape, 1925.

Wilkinson, Henry Spenser. *Thirty-five Years: 1874–1909*. London: Constable, 1933.

Winnington-Ingram, H. F. *Hearts of Oak*. London: Allen, 1889.

Poetry, Songs, and Fiction

Browning, Robert. *Poetical Works, 1833–1864*. London: Oxford, 1970.

Bullen, Frank T. *Idylls of the Sea and Other Marine Stories*. London: Grant Richards, 1899.

Clowes, W. Laird. *Told to the Marines*. London: Traherne, 1902.

———, and Burgoyne, Alan H. *Trafalgar Refought*. London: Nelson [1905].

Coate, H. E. Acraman. *Aliens Afloat: A Story of the Sea*. London: Stock, 1900.

Conrad, Joseph. *Lord Jim: A Tale*. New York: Heritage, 1959.

———. *Tales of Land and Sea*. New York: Hanover, 1953.

———. *Twixt Land and Sea*. New York: Doubleday, Page, 1923.

Fenn, G. Manville et al. *Stories of the Sea*. London: Nister [1912].

Frothingham, Robert, ed. *Songs of the Sea and Sailors' Chanteys: An Anthology*. Cambridge, Mass.: Houghton Mifflin, 1924.

Hayens, Herbert, ed. *The Imperial Adventure Book*. London: Collins, [1919].

Hopkins, Gerard Manley, *Poems*. 3d ed. London: Oxford, 1948.

Kingsley, Charles. *Hereward the Wake: "Last of the English."* 2 vols. London: Macmillan, 1881.

———. *Westward Ho! Or, the Voyages and Adventures of Sir Amyas Leigh, Knight, of Burrough, in the County of Devon, in the Reign of Her Most Glorious Majesty Queen Elizabeth*. New York: Macmillan, 1943.

Kipling, Rudyard. *Captains Courageous*. New York: Doubleday, Page, 1924.

———. *The Seven Seas*. New York: Doubleday, 1914.

———. *Songs of the Sea*. London: Macmillan, 1927.

———. *Verse: Definitive Edition*. New York: Doubleday, 1940.

Lawson, Cecil C. P. *Naval Ballads and Sea Songs*. London: Davies, 1933.

Long, W. H., ed. *Naval Yarns*. London: Gibbings, 1899.

Low, Charles Rathbone. *Britannia's Bulwarks: An Historical Poem, Descriptive of the Deeds of the British Navy*. London: Cox, 1895.

———. *Old England's Navy: An Epic of the Sea*. London: Stock, 1891.

Marryat, [Frederick]. *Frank Mildmay: Or the Naval Officer*. New York: Appleton, 1873.

———. *Peter Simple and the Little Savage*. Boston: Estes [1896].

Patterson, J. E., ed. *The Sea's Anthology: From Earliest Times down to the Middle of the Nineteenth Century*. London: Heinemann, 1913.

Rowell, George, ed. *Nineteenth-Century Plays*. London: Oxford, 1953.

Russell, W. Clark. *Alone on a Wide, Wide Sea*. 3 vols. London: Chatto & Windus, 1892.

———. *An Atlantic Tragedy and Other Stories*. London: Digby Long, 1905.

———. *The Captain's Wife*. Boston: Page, 1903.

———. *The Father of the Sea and Other Legends of the Deep*. 3d ed. London: Sampson Low, 1911.

———. *The Honour of the Flag and Other Stories*. London: Unwin, 1896.

———. *The Phantom Death and Other Stories*. New York: Stokes, 1895.

Sharp, Cecil, ed. *One Hundred English Folk Songs*. Boston: Oliver Ditson, 1916.

Sharp, Mrs. William, ed. *Sea-Music: An Anthology of Poems and Passages Descriptive of the Sea*. London: Scott [1888?].

Smith, Laura Alexandrine, ed. *The Music of the Waters: A Collection of the Sailors' Chanties, or Working Songs of the Sea, of All Maritime*

Nations, Boatmen's, Fisherman's and Rowing Songs, and Water Legends. London: Kegan, Paul, Trench, 1888.

Stevenson, Robert Louis. *Complete Poems.* New York: Scribner, 1923.

Swinburne, Algernon Charles. *Poems.* 6 vols. New York and London: Harper, 1904.

———. *A Word for the Navy.* London: Redway, 1887.

Tennyson, Alfred. *Poetic and Dramatic Works.* Cambridge ed. Boston and New York: Houghton Mifflin, 1898.

Williamson, W. M., ed. *The Eternal Sea: An Anthology of Sea Poetry.* New York: Coward-McCann, 1946.

Woodroofe, Thomas, ed. *Best Stories of the Sea.* London: Faber, 1945.

Children's Literature

The distinction between what adults and children read is not always clear, but some books are explicitly for the young. As I noted earlier, these tend to be openly moral or didactic in tone. Included below are stories, novels, poetry, and essays, but not histories, which were grouped under histories.

Boy's Own Sea Stories: Being the Adventures of a Sailor in the Navy, the Merchant Service, and on a Whaling Cruise, "Narrated by Himself." London: Ward, Lock [1880].

Bullen, Frank T. *A Son of the Sea.* London: Nisbet, 1905.

Crofts, Cecil H. *Britain on and beyond the Sea: A Handbook to the Navy League Map of the World.* Edinburgh: Johnston [1900].

Hadden, J. Cuthbert. *The Boy's Book of the Navy: Its Ships and Its Services.* London: Partridge [1911]

———. *The Boy's Life of Nelson.* London: Partridge [1905].

———. *Stirring Sea Fights: A Book for British Boys.* London: Partridge [1908].

Hayens, Herbert. *Stirring and True.* London: Collins [1907].

———. *Two Old Sea-Dogs: Drake and Blake.* London: Collins [1904].

———. *Ye Mariners of England: A Boy's Book of the Navy* London: Nelson, 1901.

Kingston, W. H. G. *My First Voyage to Southern Seas: A Book for Boys.* London: Nelson, 1874.

Knollys, W., and Elliott, W. J. *Dashing Deeds Afloat and Ashore.* London: Dean [1892].

———. *Hearts of Oak Exploits: Or, Sailor Heroes.* London: Dean [1897].

Laughton, John Knox. *Sea Fights and Adventures.* London: Allen, 1901.

Low, Charles Rathbone. *England's Sea Victories.* London: Virtue, 1893.

———. *Tales of Naval Adventure.* London: Routledge, 1872.

172

Macaulay, [James]. *All True: Records of Peril and Adventure by Sea and Land—Remarkable Escapes and Deliverances—Missionary Enterprises —Wonders of Nature and Providence—Incidents of Christian History and Biography; a Book of Sunday Reading for the Young.* London: Hodder & Stoughton, 1879.

——. *Thrilling Tales of Enterprise and Peril, Adventure and Heroism.* London: Hodder & Stoughton, 1886.

——. *Wonderful Stories of Daring, Enterprise, and Adventure.* London: Hodder & Stoughton, 1887.

Shaw, Frank H. *In the Days of Nelson: A Story of the Battle of the Nile.* London: Cassell [1910].

——. *Keepers of the Sea.* London: Cassell [1919].

——. *Sons of the Sea: A Story for Boys.* London: Cassell [1912].

Wyatt, G. E. *Follow the Right: A Tale for Boys.* London: Nelson, 1890.

JOURNALISTIC SOURCES

Pamphlets

There was a considerable amount of pamphlet literature in this period, probably far more than is published today. The following were the most useful; some of them were reprinted from other sources.

Bedford, F. G. D. *Life on Board H.M.S. "Britannia."* Portsmouth: Gieve [1919].

Brassey, T. *Naval Reserves.* London: Mitchell [1874].

Cornish, Thomas. *Losses of Life at Sea and the Means of Averting Such Calamities.* London: Railway, 1882.

Elliott, Charles: *A Proposal in Behalf of the Seamen of the Kingdom.* London: Ridgway, 1852.

——. *A Plan for the Formation of a Maritime Militia or Sea Fencible Force in a Letter to the Right Honorable the Earl of Derby.* London: Ridgway, 1852.

Laughton, J. K. *The Story of Trafalgar.* Portsmouth: Griffin, 1890.

Lennox, Henry. *Forewarned, Forearmed.* London: Ridgway, 1882.

[Martin, William]. *The Admiralty.* 2d ed. Portsmouth: Griffin, 1870.

Matheson, P. E. *National Ideals.* Oxford: Oxford Univ. Press [1915].

McHardy, C. McL. *The British Navy for One Hundred Years.* London: Navy League, 1896.

Neptune [pseud.]. *Our Naval Policy.* London: Freethought, 1886.

[Pakington, J.]. *A Clear Anchor: The Board of Admiralty, Can it not be Reformed, or Must it be Wholly Reconstructed?* 2d ed. London: Harrison, 1871.

Reed, E. J. *The State of the Navy.* London: National Union, 1885.

Robinson, R. Spencer. *Admiralty Reform: The Necessity for Undertaking It and the Direction That Should Be Given It.* London: Harrison, 1886.

————. *On the State of the British Navy: With Remarks on One Branch of Naval Expenditure.* London: Harrison, 1874.

Russell, W. Clark. *A Forecastle View of the Shipping Commission.* London: Sampson, Low, 1885.

The Story of the Battle of Port Said: A Chapter in the History of the Future. London: Engineering, 1883.

Thursfield, J. R. *The Navy and the War.* Oxford: Oxford Univ Press, 1914.

Wilkinson, Spenser. *The Brain of the Navy.* London: Constable, 1895.

————. *The Secret of the Sea: A Chapter Extracted from the Great Alternative, a Plea for a National Policy.* London: Swan, Sonnenschein, 1895.

Wyatt, H. F., and Horton-Smith, L.G.H. *Britain's Imminent Danger.* 2d ed. London: Imperial Maritime League, 1912.

————. *The Truth about the Navy.* London: Sampson, Low, n.d.

Journals and Reviews

The files of the following periodicals have been useful. For details on individual articles, see the notes to the chapters. Children's journals are included here.

At Home and Abroad
Blackwood's
Boy's Library
Boys of the British Empire
Boys of the Nation
Boys' Own Journal
Boys' Own Reader
Cassell's Family Magazine
Comrades
Contemporary Review
Cornhill
Fortnightly Review
Gentleman's Magazine
Illustrated London News
Macmillan's
Mariner's Mirror
Monthly Review
National Review
Nautical Magazine
Nautical Magazine and Naval Chronicle
Naval and Military Magazine
Navy League Annual

Navy League Quarterly
Nineteenth Century
Nineteenth Century and After
New Review
Pearson's Magazine
Quarterly Review
Transactions of the Royal Historical Society
United Service Institution Record
United Service Magazine
United Service Magazine and Military Journal
Wide World Magazine

Newspapers

Daily Chronicle
Daily Mail
Daily News
Daily Telegraph
Echo
Evening News
Globe
Manchester Guardian
Morning
Morning Post
Pall Mall Gazette
Standard
St. James Gazette
Times

NOTES

In the interests of simplicity, I have omitted notes for titled poems of well-known authors.

CHAPTER 1

1. Robert Graves, *The Greek Myths*, 1:10.
2. E. B. Tyler, *Primitive Culture*, 1:276. Professor Otten, in discussing Thomas B. Macaulay's theory of poetry, treats the notion that primitive ages are by nature more poetic because they are more metaphoric. Macaulay believed that imaginative poetry developed early and rapidly in the history of a culture, whereas analytical sciences advanced more slowly and cumulatively. Basically, Macaulay assumed the incompatibility of imagination and reason; I would be more inclined to call them symbiotic (*South Atlantic Quarterly* 72 (Spring 1973): 280–94).
3. C. G. Jung, *Collected Works*, 9:43.
4. Mircea Eliade, *Patterns in Comparative Religion*, p. 431. For further analysis of the science-myth question see Ernst Cassirer, *Language and Myth*; and Susanne K. Langer, *Philosophy in a New Key*.
5. Bronislaw Malinowski, *Magic, Science, and Religion, and Other Essays*, pp. 122 and 78.
6. Quoted in Henry Murray, *Myth and Mythmaking*, p. 359.

CHAPTER 2

1. Jerome Hamilton Buckley, *The Victorian Temper*, chap. 5.
2. Mrs. William Sharp, *Sea-Music*, p. 103.
3. Quoted in Christopher Lloyd, *Captain Marryat and the Old Navy*, p. vii. See also Gerard Jean-Aubry, *The Sea Dreamer: A Definitive Biography of Joseph Conrad*.
4. Joseph Conrad, *The Mirror of the Sea*, p. viii.
5. Ibid., p. x.
6. J. E. Patterson, *The Sea's Anthology*, p. xxi.

7. Conrad, *Mirror of the Sea*, p. 135.
8. Ibid., pp. 141–42, and 148.
9. Ibid., p. 148.
10. Kipling, *Verse*, p. 171; and Sharp, *Sea-Music*, pp. 290 and 291.
11. H. E. Acraman Coate, *Realities of Sea Life*, p. vii.
12. Conrad, *Mirror of the Sea*, p. 56; and Joseph Conrad, *Twixt Land and Sea*, p. 96.
13. Conrad, *Mirror of the Sea*, p. 56.
14. Ibid., p. 30.
15. Ibid., pp. 91–101.
16. Buckley, *Victorian Temper*, p. 88.
17. George Eliot, *Impressions of Theophrastus Such* (Boston: Houghton Mifflin, n.d.), p. 188.

CHAPTER 3

1. Cleanth Brooks, *The Well-Wrought Urn*, pp. 164–65.
2. John Knox Laughton, "The National Study of Naval History," *Transactions Royal Historical Society* n.s. 12 (1898): 86.
3. [Robert Louis Stevenson], "The English Admirals," *Cornhill* 38 (July 1878):36.
4. Ibid.
5. J. Cuthbert Hadden, *The Boy's Life of Nelson*, p. 12.
6. Spenser Wilkinson, *The Secret of the Sea*, p. 2.
7. Herbert Hayens, *Ye Mariners of England*, p. 10; C. H. Wyatt, *English Citizen*, p. 170; E. A. Freeman, "Latest Theories on the Origin of the English," *Contemporary Review* 57 (January 1890): 45; and James Anthony Froude, *Oceana*, p. 14.
8. *The Story of Greater Britain*, p. 196; and Frank T. Bullen, *Our Heritage of the Sea*, pp. 303–6, and xx.
9. J. Cuthbert Hadden, *The Boy's Book of the Navy*, p. 49; and Agnes Giberne, *The Romance of the Mighty Deep*, p. 4.
10. W. Clark Russell, *The Father of the Sea, and Other Legends of the Deep*, pp. 25–26.
11. W. C. Sellar and R. J. Yeatman, *1066 and All That*, p. 11; and Giberne, *Romance of the Mighty Deep*, p. 263.
12. Frank Fox, *Ramparts of Empire*, pp. 32–33. Fox was a citizen of one of the overseas dominions (probably Australia), but his dedication to the English myth was warm and devout.
13. H. F. Wyatt and L. G. H. Horton-Smith, *The Passing of the Great Fleet*, p. xiv. See also W. Clarke Hall and Clement Salaman, *Britain's Glory*, p. 12.
14. John Knox Laughton, *From Howard to Nelson*, pp. v–vi.
15. Charles Rathbone Low, *England's Sea Victories*, p. v; *Daily Telegraph*, 12 June 1897; and Evelyn Baring, *Ancient and Modern Imperialism* (New York: Longmans, Green, 1910), p. 113 and passim.

16. Christopher Lloyd, *The Nation and the Navy*, pp. 224-25.
17. Richard Holland, "How Ships Are Spoken at Sea," *Cassell's* (September 1888): 609-11; and C. N. Robinson, *The British Fleet*, p. 83.
18. C. W. C. Oman, *An Elementary History of Greece*, p. 88; and Arthur S. Walpole, *Little Arthur's History of Greece*, p. 105 (this volume is part of a series of Little Arthur's histories, written for young children and deliberately didactic and exciting. The preface emphasizes that stories without a hero are not easy for children to remember, and thus the stress would be on the heroic).
19. A. H. Allcroft, *Making of Athens, a History of Greece*, p. 58; Walpole, *Little Arthur's History of Greece*, p. 122; and Maria Callcott, *Little Arthur's History of England*, p. 184.
20. J. B. Bury, *History of Greece for Beginners*, pp. 154-55. This book was an abridgement for school-age children of his larger *History of Greece*, published in 1900. See also his remarks on the Greek view of life in the introduction to *The Idea of Progress*.
21. C. H. Crofts, *Britain on and beyond the Sea*, p. 28.
22. A Naval Peer [pseud.], *Our Naval Position and Policy*, p. 176; and Herbert Hayens, *The Story of Europe*, p. 192.
23. J. E. Patterson, *Sea's Anthology*, p. 235.
24. Sellar and Yeatman, *1066 and All That*, p. 11; and *Navy League Annual* (1896), p. 150.
25. Navy League, pamphlet no. C-4 [1896], p. 4.
26. Alfred Tennyson, *Poetic and Dramatic Works*, p. 525.

CHAPTER 4

1. W. H. Auden, *The Enchaféd Flood*, p. 21. Auden discusses a host of garden-paradise-island images in English and classical literature.
2. E. A. Freeman, "Alter Orbis," *Contemporary Review* 41 (June 1882): 1042-43 and passim.
3. Ibid., p. 1043.
4. Ibid., p. 1046.
5. E. A. Freeman, *Comparative Politics* (London: [Cambridge Univ. Press?], 1874), p. 352.
6. Ibid.
7. Freeman, "Alter Orbis," p. 1049.
8. Ibid., p. 1050.
9. Edward A. Freeman, "Continuity of English History," in *Historical Essays*, p. 51.
10. Ford Madox Ford, *England and the English*, pp. 256-58.
11. Charles N. Robinson, *The British Fleet*, p. 51; and Frederick Greenwood, "The Wilful Isolation of England," *Contemporary Review* 67 (June 1895): 840-41.
12. "England and the Powers," *Monthly Review* 6 (March 1902): 2-3.

NOTES

13. W. Boyd Dawkins, "The 'Silver Streak' and the Channel Tunnel," *Contemporary Review* 43 (February 1883): 244.
14. "England and the Powers," *Monthly Review* 6:3.
15. Mrs. William Sharp, *Sea-Music*, p. xx. Historians like John R. Seeley (*The Expansion of England*) and James Froude (*Oceana*) also popularized this idea.
16. Marquis of Halifax, *A Rough Draft of a New Model at Sea*, quoted in Frederick Page, *An Anthology of Patriotic Prose* (London: Oxford University Press, 1915), pp. 185–86.
17. [W. E. Gladstone], "Germany, France, and England," *Edinburgh Review* 132 (October 1870): 555–93.
18. Alfred Austin, "Three Sonnets: Written in mid-Channel," *Contemporary Review* 41 (June 1882): 1039–40.
19. Charles N. Robinson and John Leyland, *For the Honour of the Flag*, p. 356.
20. Quoted in Thomas Whiteside, *The Tunnel under the Channel*, p. 6. This book, an extraordinarily interesting account of the history of tunnel schemes, is thorough, and I have relied on much of its information. The cartoon is from *Punch*, reprinted in Whiteside, *Tunnel*, p. 31.
21. Austin, "Three Sonnets," pp. 1039–40.
22. Sharp, *Sea-Music*, p. xx.
23. P. H. Ditchfield, "Where Will the Enemy Land?" *Pearson's Magazine* (February 1910): 163-72. The date is perhaps significant.
24. Charles N. Robinson, *Sea Service*, n.p.; and A Naval Peer [pseud.], *Our Naval Position and Policy*, chap. 13.
25. Whiteside, *Tunnel under the Channel*, p. 9.
26. Quoted in ibid., p. 23.
27. *Times* (London), 18 June 1881.
28. Admiral Lord Dunsany, "The 'Silver Streak,'" *Nineteenth Century* 9 (May 1881): 735–55; 11 (February 1882): 288–304; and Lord Brabourne, "The Channel Tunnel," *Contemporary Review* 41 (March 1882): 527.
29. Lord Brabourne, "The Channel Tunnel," p. 527.
30. *Standard*, 20 February 1882; *Manchester Guardian*, 31 January 1882.
31. *Pall Mall Gazette*, 16 March 1882; *Daily News*, 30 January 1882.
32. *Times* (London), 16 October 1882.
33. *Standard*, 21 February 1882.
34. Freeman, "Alter Orbis," p. 1042; and *Times* (London), quoted in Whiteside, *Tunnel under the Channel*, p. 43.

CHAPTER 5

1. E. A. Freeman, "Latest Theories on the Origin of the English," *Contemporary Review* 57 (January 1890): 36; and James Anthony Froude, *Oceana*, p. 14.
2. John Knox Laughton, *Study of Naval History*, p. 5. Palmerston is

180

quoted by Charles R. Low in *Great Battles of the British Navy*, pp. vii–viii.

3. W. Clarke Hall and Clement Salaman, *Britain's Glory*, p. 56; and Michael Lewis, *England's Sea-Officers*, p. 24.

4. Hall and Salaman, *Britain's Glory*, p. 11; and Herbert Hayens, *Ye Mariners of England*, p. 434.

5. C. McL. McHardy, *British Seamen*, p. 7; and Low, *Great Battles of the British Navy*, p. 493.

6. Hayens, *Ye Mariners of England*, p. 207.

7. W. Knollys and W. J. Elliott, *Hearts of Oak Exploits*, p. 202.

8. W. Knollys and W. J. Elliott, *Dashing Deeds Afloat and Ashore*, p. 29.

9. Herbert Hayens, *Two Old Seadogs*, p. 152; and Hayens, *Ye Mariners of England*, p. 51.

10. Fred T. Jane, "The Navy—Is All Well?" *Fortnightly Review* n.s. 71 (March 1902): 457.

11. Probably the most vivid account of this incident, which is related in many places, is in Q., *Story of the Sea*, 1: 80–82.

12. [G. W. Steevens], "Recent Naval Biography and Criticism," *Blackwood's* 161 (March 1897): 412; and Spenser Wilkinson, *Brain of the Navy*, p. 96.

13. Spenser Wilkinson, *The Great Alternative*, p. 327.

14. Hayens, *Seadogs*, pp. 187 and 188.

15. G. Quick, "The Defense of the British Empire: the Duty of Every British Boy," *Navy League Quarterly*, no. 12 (April 1913), p. 5.

16. *Comrades* 1 (17 January 1898).

17. "The British Seaman: Then and Now," *Navy League Quarterly*, no. 5 (July 1911), pp. 35–36.

18. "The Coasts of High Barbary," in *English Folk-Songs*, ed. Cecil J. Sharp, p. 32.

19. Knollys and Elliott, *Hearts of Oak*, p. 197.

20. Q., *Story of the Sea*, 1: 743. Russell is quoted in Mrs. William Sharp, *Sea-Music*, p. xxi.

21. Christopher Lloyd, *The Nation and the Navy*, p. 155; and J. E. Patterson, *The Sea's Anthology*, pp. 190-91.

22. Charles Dibdin's "The Flowing Can" is in *Naval Ballads and Sea Songs*, ed. Cecil C. P. Lawson, p. 40.

23. John Knox Laughton, *Sea Fights and Adventures*, p. 231.

24. Henry McDonald, "A Minor Operation: A Story of Modern Warfare," *Pearson's* 37 (January 1914): 79-88.

25. Frank H. Mason, *The Book of British Ships*, p. 349; and the *Times* (London), 19 July 1902.

26. "A Few Words on the Royal Navy," Navy League pamphlet no. C-4 (1896), p. 3.

27. H. A., "Tom Giles; An Account of an Episode in the Life of a City Lad," *Navy League Quarterly* May 1910, pp. 5-6.

28. Vernon W. Anson, "The Training of Boys for the Navy," *Navy League Annual* (1896), pp. 174–75; and Board of Admiralty, *The Entry and Training of Naval Cadets*, pp. 1–2.

29. Spenser Wilkinson, *The Nation's Need*, pp. 280–81.

30. See, for example, Hall and Salaman, *Britain's Glory*, p. 59. See also a poem of Kipling's called "The Scholars" and [Frederick] Whymper, *The Sea*, 3:46.

31. G. W. Steevens, *Naval Policy*, Chap. 7.

32. Charles Rathbone Low, *Britannia's Bulwarks*, p. 416; and McHardy, *British Seamen*, p. 18.

33. James Macaulay, *Thrilling Tales of Enterprise and Peril, Adventure and Heroism*, pp. 72–73.

34. W. Cains Crutchley, "The Needs of the Mercantile Marine," *Navy League Annual* (1896), pp. 162–64; and W. Clark Russell, *Pictures from the Life of Nelson*, preface, pp. vi–vii.

35. Steevens, *Naval Policy*, pp. 214–17; Walter Jeffery, *A Century of Our Sea Story*, pp. 265–66; and F. T. Jane, *Imperial Russian Navy*, pp. 565–67.

36. W. H. Davenport Adams, *Eminent Sailors*, pp. vii–viii; and W. Laird Clowes, *All About the Royal Navy*, p. 91.

37. *Standard*, 3 February 1912.

38. G. E. Armstrong, *Torpedoes and Torpedo Vessels*, pp. 5–6.

39. Charles Napier Robinson, *The British Tar in Fact and Fiction*, preface.

40. [Robert Louis Stevenson], "The English Admirals," *Cornhill* 38 (July 1878): 36.

41. S. Eardley-Wilmot, "The Navy as a Profession," Navy League pamphlet no. F-1 (1896), p. 4.

CHAPTER 6

1. James Anthony Froude, *English Seamen in the Sixteenth Century*, p. 30.

2. H. R. Fox Bourne, *English Seamen under the Tudors*, 2:222.

3. Froude, *English Seamen*, p. 255.

4. Maria Callcott, *Little Arthur's History of England*, p. 181; and Froude, *English Seamen*, p. 257.

5. Froude, *English Seamen*, p. 257.

6. W. H. Davenport Adams, *England on the Sea*, 1:87.

7. Frank H. Shaw and Ernest H. Robinson, *The Sea and Its Story*, p. 10; J. K. Laughton, "Howard," in *From Howard to Nelson*, p. 25; and Frank Fox, *Ramparts of Empire*, p. 37.

8. Adams, *England on the Sea*, 1: 77 and 80.

9. Froude, *English Seamen*, p. 32; Herbert Hayens, *Ye Mariners of England*, p. 33; Herbert Hayens, *Two Old Sea Dogs*, p. 62; and Cecil H. Crofts, *Britain on and beyond the Sea*, pp. 2 and 1.

10. E. P. Statham, *Privateers and Privateering*, p. 3; Froude, *English Seamen*, p. 32; and Shaw and Robinson, *The Sea and Its Story*, p. 9 and passim.

11. Adams, *England on the Sea*, 1:60; Frank H. Mason, *The Book of British Ships*, p. 43; and Bourne, *English Seamen under the Tudors*, 2: 25 and 17.

12. C. McL. McHardy, *The British Empire*, pp. 7-8; and Bourne, *English Seamen under the Tudors*, 2:127.

13. Charles N. Robinson, "Defeat of the Armada in 1588," *Illustrated London News*, 14 July 1888; and Frederick G. P. Bedford, "Drake," in Laughton, *From Howard to Nelson*, p. 80.

14. Fox, *Ramparts of Empire*, p. 35.

15. Quoted in ibid.

16. C. H. Wyatt, *The English Citizen*, p. 172; Charles Rathbone Low, *Her Majesty's Navy*, 1:16; and Charles Rathbone Low, *England's Sea Victories*, pp. 14-15.

17. Froude, *English Seamen*, pp. 263-65.

18. Charles Kingsley, *Westward Ho!*, p. 323.

19. Charles Dickens, *A Child's History of England*, p. 228.

20. Calcott, *Little Arthur's History of England*, p. 184; C. N. Robinson, *Illustrated London News*, 14 July 1888; and Bedford, "Drake," p. 80.

21. Froude, *English Seamen*, p. 308; and *Pall Mall Gazette*, 23 October 1905.

22. Froude, *English Seamen*, p. 309.

CHAPTER 7

1. Thomas Carlyle, *Heroes, Hero-Worship, and the Heroic in History* (London: Chapman and Hall, 1897), p. 13.

2. Charles Kingsley, *Health and Education*, pp. 205 and 203.

3. Ibid., pp. 208 and 210.

4. Ibid., p. 217.

5. Robert Southey, *The Life of Horatio Lord Nelson*; and Sir N. Harris Nicolas, *The Dispatches and Letters of Vice-Admiral Lord Viscount Nelson*.

6. Charles Rathbone Low, *Her Majesty's Navy*, 3: 170.

7. *Pall Mall Gazette*, 21 October 1905; and [Frederick] Whymper, *The Sea*, 1:ii.

8. Low, *Her Majesty's Navy*, 3:22.

9. *Daily Mail*, 21 October 1905; J. Cuthbert Hadden, *The Boy's Life of Nelson*, p. 17; and Q., *Story of the Sea*, 1:34.

10. John Knox Laughton, *Nelson*, p. 48; and J. K. Laughton, *The Story of Trafalgar*, p. 39.

11. Nelson is quoted in W. Clark Russell, *Pictures from the Life of Nelson*, p. 50; Frank H. Shaw, *In The Days of Nelson; A Story of the Battle of the Nile*; and *Manchester Guardian* 21 October 1905.

12. Among others, Southey, *The Life of Nelson*, 2:285.
13. Philip H. Colomb, "Nelson," in Laughton, *From Howard to Nelson*, pp. 453 and 459.
14. J. K. Laughton, *Nelson and His Companions in Arms*, p. 81. See also Herbert Hayens, *Ye Mariners of England*, pp. 196–97.
15. Colomb, "Nelson," p. 448.
16. Russell, *Pictures*, p. 120.
17. Laughton, *Nelson and His Companions in Arms*, p. 140; and Russell, *Pictures*, p. 131.
18. Ibid., p. 312.
19. Low, *Her Majesty's Navy*, 3:171.
20. Lord Rosebery, "Nelson," in *Miscellanies*, 2:20.
21. Russell, *Pictures*, p. 46.
22. J. Cuthbert Hadden, *Stirring Sea Fights*, p. 326; W. Clark Russell, *Nelson's Words and Deeds*, p. 146; Laughton, *Story of Trafalgar*, p. 3; and Low, *Her Majesty's Navy*, 3:26.
23. C. H. Wyatt, *The English Citizen*, p. 174; and J. K. Laughton, "The Centennial of Trafalgar," *Quarterly Review* 203 (October 1905): 630.
24. Charles Rathbone Low, *England's Sea Victories*, p. 236 (this is in fact the last sentence of the book); and Laughton, *Story of Trafalgar*, p. 40.
25. W. Laird Clowes and Alan H. Burgoyne, *Trafalgar Refought*.
26. *Manchester Guardian*, 21 October 1905; and Russell, *Nelson's Words and Deeds*, p. vii.
27. Reprinted in Rosebery, *Miscellanies*, 2:18–19.
28. W. H. Davenport Adams, *England on the Sea*, 2:190; and *Pall Mall Gazette*, 21 October 1905.
29. Frank H. Shaw, *Keepers of the Sea*, p. 21; Whymper, *The Sea*, 1:13; and C. R. L. Fletcher and Rudyard Kipling, *A School History of England*, p. 214 (Kipling wrote the poems which are appended to each chapter).
30. Rosebery, *Miscellanies*, 2:21; and Russell, *Pictures*, p. 316.

CHAPTER 8

1. Spenser Wilkinson, *Britain at Bay*, chap. 8 ("Nationhood Neglected"); and the *Globe*, 11 June 1897.
2. H. F. Wyatt and L. G. H. Horton-Smith, *Britain's Imminent Danger*, pp. 8–9; H. F. Wyatt and L. G. H. Horton-Smith, *The Passing of the Great Fleet*, p. xi; and H. F. Wyatt, *God's Test by War*, pp. 27 and 48.
3. John Ruskin, "Lectures on Art," *Collected Works*, 4:216; and Agnes Giberne, *The Romance of the Mighty Deep*, p. 289.
4. Herbert Hayens, *The Story of Europe*, pp. 189–90; and *Naval and Military Magazine* 1 (July 1897): 110.
5. R. B. Mowat, *The Victorian Age*, p. 228.

6. Mowat, *Victorian Age*, p. 228; and Charles Wentworth Dilke and Spenser Wilkinson, *Imperial Defence*, pp. 42–43.

7. Charles Rathbone Low, "History of the Indian Navy," *United Service Magazine* (January 1878): 65; and Dilke and Wilkinson, *Imperial Defence*, pp. 37–38.

8. The Right Honorable the Earl of Meath, "The Navy and the Empire," *Navy League Annual* (1907), p. 79.

9. John Leyland, *The Achievement of the British Navy in the World War*, pp. 88 and 95.

10. W. MacNeile Dixon, *The British Navy at War*, chap. 9.

11. Quoted in Navy League, *Guide to the Naval Review*.

12. Spenser Wilkinson, "Freedom of the Seas," in Wilkinson, *British Aspects of War and Peace*, p. 9.

13. Mowat, *Victorian Age*, pp. 226–27.

14. Sidney M. Eardley-Wilmot, *An Admiral's Memories*, pp. 172–73.

15. Frank T. Bullen, *Idylls of the Sea and Other Marine Sketches*, pp. 21–23.

16. Quoted in Christopher Lloyd, *A Short History of the Royal Navy*, pp. 50–51. Earlier quotation is from Walter Jeffrey, *A Century of Our Sea Story*, p. 109.

17. Henry Moore, *The British and American Navies*, p. 13.

18. Mowat, *Victorian Age*, p. 231; and Wilkinson, "Freedom of the Seas," pp. 17–18.

19. Eardley-Wilmot, *An Admiral's Memories*, chap. 15.

20. Herbert Hayens, *Ye Mariners of England*, p. 437; and H. W. Wilson, in Navy League pamphlet no. C-2 (May 1895).

21. Charles Rathbone Low, *Old England's Navy*, p. 127.

22. Alfred Noyes, "The Sea," in *The English Genius*, ed. H. S. Kingsmill (London: Eyre and Spottiswoode, 1938), p. 171.

23. Henry Spenser Wilkinson, *Thirty-five Years*, p. vii. This is Wilkinson's autobiography, from which most of the material here has been taken.

24. Ibid., p. vii.

25. Ibid., pp. 185–87.

26. Spenser Wilkinson, *The Great Alternative*, p. 297.

27. Q., *The Story of the Sea*, 1:3; Seton Karr, *Minutes of the Proceedings at the Navy League Conference to Consider the Position of This Country If Involved in War*, pp. 65–91; and Ernest Williams, *Minutes of the Navy League Meeting*, p. 74.

28. *The Mercantile Marine in Wartime*, pp. 48–49 (articles reprinted from the *Shipping and Mercantile Gazette* arguing for more efficiency and an armed mercantile marine); and H. W. Wilson, "The Needs of the Navy," *Naval and Military Magazine* 2 (February 1898): 56.

29. "Is Invasion Impossible?" *Nautical Magazine* 81 (April 1909): 304; Wilkinson, "Freedom of the Seas," p. 15; and C. R. Low, *Her Majesty's Navy*, 1:v.

30. Mowat, *Victorian Age*, p. 227. It is interesting that this book was published in 1939, only a year before the threat of German invasion became for once a serious possibility.

31. Dilke and Wilkinson, *Imperial Defence*, p. 42; *Morning Post*, 20 February 1896; and Admiral Mahan, quoted in Wilkinson, *Britain at Bay*, p. 41.

32. Wilson, "Needs of the Navy," pp. 55 and 56; and Herbert Richmond, *Statesmen and Seapower*, pp. 270-71.

33. Spenser Wilkinson, *The Secret of the Sea*, pp. 24-27.

34. Spenser Wilkinson, *The Nation's Awakening*, p. 276; and Wilkinson, *The Command of the Sea*, pp. 59-60.

35. Charles Elliott, *A Plan for the Formation of a Maritime Militia or Sea Fencible Force*, p. 1.

36. [C.C.P. Fitzgerald], "The Balance of Power in Europe: Its Naval Aspect," *Blackwood's* 143 (February 1888): 291.

37. *The Story of the Battle of Port Said* (first published as an article in the journal *Engineering*); and Low, *Her Majesty's Navy*, 1:v.

38. Wilkinson, *Britain at Bay*, see especially chap. 7; "Another War Note," *Nautical Magazine* 81 (February 1909): 151; and John T. Middlemore, *The Navy in the House of Commons*, p. v.

39. Wilkinson, *The Secret of the Sea*, pp. 11-13; and Thomas Gibson Bowles, *Sea Law and Sea Power*, pp. 9-12.

40. Michael Cababé, *The Freedom of the Seas*, p. 19 and passim.

41. *The Mercantile Marine in Wartime*, p. 8; and *Evening News*, 5 October 1899.

42. Spenser Wilkinson, *Morning Post*, 20 February 1896; and *Command of the Sea*, pp. 31-37.

43. Wilkinson, *Britain at Bay*, chaps. 3 and 4.

44. Wilkinson, *Command of the Sea*, pp. 61-63, 50, and 52-53.

45. Ibid., p. 3-14; and *Morning Post*, 20 February 1896.

46. [C.C.P. Fitzgerald], "Our Naval Policy," *Blackwood's* 143 (April 1888): 582-83; and [Fitzgerald], "The Balance of Power in Europe," pp. 288-89.

47. J. K. Laughton, "The National Study of Naval History," *Transactions of the Royal Historical Society*, n.s. 12 (1898): 82.

CHAPTER 9

1. *Pall Mall Gazette*, 12 March 1896; and D. M. Schurman, *The Education of a Navy*, pp. 1-2.

2. Henry G. Lennox, *Forewarned, Forearmed*, pp. 37-46.

3. [C.C.P. Fitzgerald], "The Balance of Power in Europe: Its Naval Aspect," *Blackwood's* 143 (February 1888): 285 and 286.

4. E. J. Reed, "On Cruisers," a lecture at the Royal United Service Institution, reported in the *Times* (London), 30 June 1888.

5. *Times* (London), 29 May 1888.

6. [S. J. Foley], "The Naval Manoeuvres: Their Objects and Results," *Blackwood's* 144 (September 1888): 465-74; and Reginald C. Oldknow, *The Mechanism of Men-of-War*, pp. 247-48.

7. *St. James Gazette*, 17 March 1890.

8. *Pall Mall Gazette*, 27 March 1895.

9. J. Cuthbert Hadden, *The Boy's Book of the Navy*, pp. 112-16; and W. Laird Clowes, "The Navy in the Victorian Era," *Illustrated London News*, special memorial issue (Record of the Glorious Reign of Queen Victoria), 1902, p. 54.

10. W. Laird Clowes, *All About the Royal Navy*, p. 121; and Lieutenant G. E. Armstrong, *Torpedoes and Torpedo-Vessels*, pp. ix-x (this book is the third of the series, Royal Naval Handbooks, edited by C. N. Robinson).

11. *Morning Post*, 3 March 1896; and *Globe*, 21 March 1894.

12. *St. James Gazette*, 19 March 1890; and Spenser Wilkinson, *Britain at Bay*, pp. 132-34.

13. "The Study of Naval Tactics," *United Service Magazine* (December 1881): 400.

14. Mrs. Acland, "Some Reminiscences of the Right Hon. W. H. Smith at the Admiralty," in Navy League, *Guide to the Naval Review*, pp. 3-4 (Mrs. Acland was Smith's daughter).

15. R. Spencer Robinson, *Admiralty Reform, the Necessity for Undertaking It and the Direction That Should be Given It*, p. 6 and passim.

16. [C. C. P. Fitzgerald], "Our Naval Policy," *Blackwood's* 143 (April 1888): 591; and Spenser Wilkinson in *Pall Mall Gazette*, 14 March 1895.

17. *St. James Gazette*, 24 March 1890; and *Times* (London), 30 June 1888.

18. Spenser Wilkinson, *The Command of the Sea*, p. 66.

19. *Globe*, 28 February 1894.

20. [G. W. Steevens], "The Navy Estimates," *Blackwood's* 161 (April, 1897): 570-71; and Fred T. Jane, "The Navy—Is All Well?" *Fortnightly Review* n.s. 71 (March 1902): 448-56. See also C. McL. McHardy, *The British Navy for a Hundred Years*, p. 8.

21. Tennyson revised the poem several times, and different versions were published in the newspapers and elsewhere from 1886 to 1901.

22. A good survey is Christopher Lloyd, *The Nation and the Navy*, chaps. 11 and 12. See also Leslie Gardiner, *The British Admiralty*. A bitter attack is to be found in Stanley Bonnet, *The Price of Admiralty*. Professor Arthur J. Marder's extensive studies of Fisher and the Fisher era should also be consulted.

23. The best short account of Laughton and his hand in this organization is to be found in Schurman, *The Education of a Navy*, chap. 5.

24. "The Navy," *United Service Magazine* (October 1881): 173; and Schurman, *Education of a Navy*, pp. 7-9.

25. "The Objects of the Navy League," (here somewhat condensed)

from *Minutes of the Proceedings at the Navy League Conference* (1898).

26. R. Vesey Hamilton, Navy League pamphlet (unnumbered), July 1895.

27. *Pall Mall Gazette*, 18 March 1895.

28. Quoted in Schurman, *Education of a Navy*, p. 99.

29. H. F. Wyatt and L. G. H. Horton-Smith, *The Passing of the Great Fleet*, p. xxxiii.

30. Ibid., pp. 306–13.

31. *Standard*, 1 February 1912, a speech by Capt. R. Muirhead Collins, R.N., C.M.G., official secretary for the Commonwealth of Australia in London, given to the Battersea and West Ham Companies of the Imperial Maritime League Naval Brigade. See also Wyatt and Horton-Smith, *Passing of the Great Fleet*, p. xvi.

32. "Resurrection of the Navy," in Navy League, *Guide to the Naval Review*, pp. 2–3.

33. Clowes, "Navy in the Victorian Era," pp. 49–54.

CHAPTER 10

1. Harold Nicolson, *The War Years, 1939–1945* (New York: Atheneum, 1967), pp. 171–72.